love waits in the rain

Thom M. Shuman

Copyright © 2016 Thom M. Shuman

All rights reserved.

ISBN: 1537025414
ISBN-13: 978-1537025414

DEDICATION

For Lisa

who continues to show others

the way to

safe faith spaces

ACKNOWLEDGMENTS

In the *Book of Common Worship,* there are two lectionaries offered. The first contains the readings for each Sunday and special days which make up the 3-year cycle of the Revised Common Lectionary, used by preachers throughout the world.

There is also a two-year cycle of daily readings which, perhaps, do not get as much attention. Which is a shame, for the scriptures offered provide an opportunity for all believers to become more immersed in the Old Book which is so central to our faith, our lives, our hopes. This book is one (*s'mores and holy ghost stories* is the other) which offers poem/prayers as reflections, nudges, doors into one of the readings for each day. These are offered as a form of *lectio divina,* where one spends time with a verse or more, to stimulate reflection, to help us to open our hearts to the Spirit, and to offer our lives to those around us.

First Week of Advent

Sunday

*Such is the company of those
    who seek him,
  who seek the face of the
    God of Jacob.* Psalm 24:6

when the din of the jingles
and commercials deafen us,
    you hear
  the soft sobs
  of the homeless child
  swaddled in newspaper;
when the bright colors
of the ads blind us,
    you watch
the teenagers buy more
  burgers and fries than they
  could ever eat, and turning
  down the alley, they hand
    the bags to the veterans
    whose hopes have
    shriveled like leaves;
when those around us
call us every name in the book,
     you take hold
  of us, hugging us tight
  to your heart whispering,
'don't you listen,
    my beloved;
  don't you listen
  to a single word.'

Monday

* learn to do good;
seek justice,
  rescue the oppressed,
defend the orphan,
  plead for the widow.* Isaiah 1:17

when we become
    life-long learners
    in the ancient

                        art
                of goodness;
when we spend
as much time
searching out the
                causes
                of injustice,
   as we do for
   online bargains;
when we rally
as quickly around
            the homeless
                teenager
     as we do our
     favorite team;
when we attend
the council meetings
         speaking out as
                forcefully
     for the shelters
     to open earlier
     this winter
          as we did
          demanding our
          taxes to be cut,
then
we
     will find our
     way
            back to
   you.

Tuesday

You yourselves know, brothers and sisters, that our coming to you was not in vain, 1 Thessalonians 2:1

when
      we look
   at the 16-year-old
            refugee,
     shivering at
     the bus stop,
     rubbing her swollen
                belly,
   and see

                        Mary;
when
        we watch
    the old man
    patiently showing
            his little grandchild
            how to carve
            a whistle out
            of a branch,
    and see
            Joseph;
when
        we pass
    the housekeepers (chatting
            in another language)
        in the hotel hallway
        as they wait to clean
                the bathrooms
                and pick up
                the mess we made,
    and see
            the shepherds,
then
        you will know
    your coming
            was not in
            vain.

Wednesday

So they watched him and sent spies who pretended to be honest, in order to trap him by what he said, so as to hand him over to the jurisdiction and authority of the governor. Luke 20:20

carefully breaking off
        a piece of that
        well-aged argument
            as to who's in
            and who's not,
    we place it on the
                catch,
        waiting for you
        to reach out and
            touch it, and
                SNAP!

    it takes some time,
        but eventually
        the test is filled
        with questions
      phrased in just
      the right way, so
          when the grading
          is done, we
          will know
          what chiliasm
              camp
you are in;
hearing you scurry
          around
  the attic of our souls,
      we set out the
      humane trap,
        so
that in the morning,
we can release you
  miles from where
  we believe,
      trusting you
      can't find your
         way
            back.
so many ways
    to trap you,
  persistent Jesus,
so many ways -
why don't you just
    give up?

Thursday

For this reason, when I could bear it no longer, I sent to find out about your faith; I was afraid that somehow the tempter had tempted you and that our labor had been in vain.
1 Thessalonians 3:5

sitting in the chair,
    you finger your
        worry beads,
      occasionally glancing
      out the window at the
          road

                    winding up to
                    the house, hoping
                        against hope . . .
out of the
                corner of your
        eye, you see her
        sitting in the warm
        glow of the lamp,
                knitting little booties
                and a blanket,
        softly humming under
                    her breath . . .
at the sound of the
                feet
        at the top of the
        stairs, you stand up
        as he comes
        down, his pack
        over one shoulder,
    smiling at you, with
                glistening eyes,
        whispering, 'well, I
        think it's time to go,'
and you watch him
            stride through
            the gate, shutting
        it gently, so as not to
        disturb the sign reading

Grace'R'Us

Friday

*that he looked down from
        his holy height,
    from heaven the LORD
        looked at the earth,* Psalm 102:19

in this season of
            silence,
    you ook down to
                hear
not
the endless carols repeated
    over and over and over;

    not bells jingling
        emptily in the malls;
    not rhymes about
        reindeer and rooftops;
    but
    the canticled cries
        of children whose
      bellies are full of the
        empty promises
        of politicians;
    the whispers
        of mothers, hoping
      that the expected call
      from the doctor will
        not be their
      worst fears;
    the moans
        of people who
      discover that their
         liberator
        has become
        the latest
      tyrant;
    in this season of
         silence,
      you look down to
         see
    if we
      are listening
      as well.

Saturday

For he delivers the needy
    when they call,
  the poor and those who
    have no helper. Psalm 72:12

we could
    overwhelm the table
  (and all our family)
    with a feast and all the
      trimmings,
or
    package up 30
      (or more)

            individual meals, and
                hand them out
                    to the homeless
                        folks down
                        by the river;
we could
        avert our eyes
    and walk a bit faster
        when we see the bullies
            pick on the
            unlucky kid
                    once again,
    or
        stop,
        put our arm
                on her shoulder,
        and walk off
            together;
we could
        circle the wagons,
        try to close all the borders,
        pass as many laws as possible
    to make sure that
            the outsiders
            stay there,
    or
        drop our defenses,
        open our arms,
        and welcome each person
            as our sister,
                our brother.
we could . . .
. . . or

Second Week of Advent

Sunday

Let me sing for my beloved
  my love-song concerning
    his vineyard: Isaiah 5:1a

carols cascade
        from the lips
        of third-graders

              packing shoeboxes
              for children in
                        parts of the
                        world they
                  only know from
                  web searches;
hymns are hummed
        by neighbors
        who rise before
              the sun rubs
              sleep from its
                        eyes,
          to shovel the walks
          of the family who
              just brought home
              their new baby;
piano keys are tickled
        by the arthritic fingers
        of the white-haired
              janitor who
              has just finished
              polishing the
                    gym floor
                    for tonight's
              dance.
our Beloved's
              love-songs
              are all around us
    if
              we but take
              the time to
    listen.

Monday

"There will be signs in the sun, the moon, and the stars, and on the earth distress among nations confused by the roaring of the sea and the waves." Luke 21:25

looking for signs
    in the entrails
    of the latest politician
        to be skewered,
            we may miss
        the story
            about

      the homeless fellow
       who pushed a
          family's car out of
        the snow
    and accepted only
      a 'thank you'
      as his reward;
reading the handwriting
        on the 'net
      regarding the cliff
    we lemmings
     seem to be running
         toward,
    we overlook
  the kids lined up
     at the tellers'
       windows, emptying
     their piggy banks
       for their teacher
battling cancer;
convinced that the warnings
   of that disembodied
       radio voice
    portend the end
of our sacred cows,
we ignore the songs
     composed in
the bathtub
by our grandchildren
    as they celebrate
   a l the wonder of
     the life they have.

Tuesday

> *the LORD opens the eyes*
> * of the blind.*
> *The LORD lifts up those who*
> * are bowed down;*
> *the LORD loves the*
> * righteous.* Psalm 146:8

when i am tempted
    to place myself
      in bondage to debt

in order to show
how much i love
    others,
set me free
    to give them
    myself
        instead;
when the glitter,
    the tinsel,
all the bright shiny
    got-to-have-or-elses
        cause me to
        squeeze my eyes
        tight shut,
open them, so
i can see the
    snow falling gently
    on a winter's night;
when i can only
    think that all
    the names on
    all the lists
        are the only
        ones
        that matter,
may the shepherds
stop me to tell
    (with wonder and
        delight)
    of the hope
they just met
in a bairn.

Wednesday

Then I heard the voice of the Lord saying, "Whom shall I send, and who will go for us?" And I said, "Here am I, send me!" Isaiah 6:8

of course,
    that is only
        if
    it fits into
    my busy schedule;
if
    i get to travel
    first-class

						all the way;
			if
				i am guaranteed
						an incredible
						severance package
					when you are not
					completely satisfied
						with my performance;
			if
				i am your first
							choice
						and not just
						some name picked
						out of the
							air;
all this is understood,
		correct,
				or otherwise
				i would have
			responded with a ?
not that silly
					!

Thursday

So he consented and began to look for an opportunity to betray him to them when no crowd was present. Luke 22:6

in the sacred space,
cocooned with so many
others, it is easy
to pray without ceasing,
to whisper your name in awe,
to find just the right words,
but
  at home,
  when the hammer hits my thumb,
    when the bills fall through
    the slot in the door,
      when the shadows lengthen,
  ah, how i use your name in a different way!
in the small group,
with those i promise to
share my deepest, darkest,
piety comes as part of the

book study,
earnestness is the pin in
my lapel,
faithfulness is always
the course of action,
but
  at work,
  in the cubicle, with only
  the screen to monitor me,
    it is easy to wander
    into those sites
    which shouldn't be found.
in the choir,
harmonizing with all
the other voices
in praise, wonder, joy,
and adoration, how can
i keep from singing
praises,
but
  driving home,
  in the anonymity of the car,
  what fun to crank up the speakers,
  boost the bass,
    shout the demeaning, degrading,
    rapping lyrics, until
      i rattle the souls
    of all those around me.
with no
crowd
around, how many
opportunities
abound!

Friday

A dispute also arose among them as to which one of them was to be regarded as the greatest. Luke 22:24

who is greater:
the superstar paid
millions
to bend a ball,
or
the coach who tells
her players, 'every one

on this team
plays
the same amount of time
each game'?
who makes
more of an impact:
the band that commands
hundreds of dollars
for a single ticket,
or the grandfather who,
in retirement,
spends time with his guitar
making up songs
for children?
who really
really changes lives:
the television PhD
whose sole focus
is ratings,
or the doctor who
travels to Central America
for a month every year
to treat folks without
charge?
when it comes to
greatness, we still use an
outdated
measuring stick,
don't we?

Saturday

He said to them, "When I sent you out without a purse, bag, or sandals, did you lack anything?" They said, "No, not a thing."
Luke 22:35

if only
    we could attract
    20-25 families
        (with 2.7
      kids each),
   then . . .
if only
    someone would
    drop the winning

        lottery ticket
        in the plate
           this week,
    then . . .
if only
   we didn't have
   so many needy
      calling and
      dropping by
         the church,
    then . . .
if only
   we got paid more
   than we're worth
      so we can
      have more
      that we want,
    then . . .
we truly won't
      lack
   anything,
      right?

Third Week of Advent

Sunday

Lead me in your truth, and
      teach me,
  for you are the God of my
      salvation,
  for you I wait all day long. Psalm 25:5

i waited
      for you
  at the coffee shop
  this morning, until
    the foam started
    to congeal in the
    cup i ordered for you,
      but the only person
      who came in was an
        out-of-work
        mom picking up
        an application;

i waitec
    for you
 down at the corner,
   finally hailing a taxi,
    if only to get
     away from that widower
      who wanted
       to bore me with
        another story about
        another grandchild,
 whi e his Golden
 sat at his feet, her eyes
  never leaving his voice;
i waited
    for you
 at the pub, munching
    the stale peanuts
    chased by the
    flattening lager,
  finally pushing off
  the stool, throwing a
   bill on the counter
   for the bartender
    who must have
    been a glutton
    for punishment,

 after listening to my
 complaints all night
  (yet, gave me a
  wistful smile as
    I left);
maybe
   tomorrow,
  you'll show up.

(The readings below are interrupted after December 17 in favor of readings identified by date in the 4th week of Advent)

Monday

I waited patiently for the
    LORD; Psalm 40:1

tap, tap,
    tapping first
    one foot and
      then the other,
  in the lingering line
    that seems to
    move slower
    with every twitch,
        i try . . .
run, run,
    running from
    one meeting to
      the next, my
    every moment
    controlled by
    relentless
      rushing time,
        i try . . .
pace, pace,
    pacing the
    hallways lined
      with worries, another
    portrait of my
    distraught soul
      being hung on
    the wall,
        i try . . .

Tuesday

Therefore I intend to keep reminding you of these things, though you know them already and are established in the truth that has come to you. 2 Peter 1:12

the prisoner
sharing his cell with
    the yellow lab,
  preparing her for
  a life of service
  to a little boy
    clinging to life
    this night . . .
the nurse
returning to her unit
    after her shift
        ends,

just in case
the little boy
who's afraid of
    dying,
awakens in the
middle of the night
  crying out for
  his mommy . . .
the soldier
sitting in the airport
    lounge,
  clutching her
  3rd cup of
   stone-cold
    coffee,
her heart a thousand
miles away,
  as she waits for
  a stand-by flight
   trying to get
   home . . .
never stop reminding
    us
that you keep
  coming to
    us . . .

Wednesday

As it is written in the prophet Isaiah:
  "See, I am sending my
    messenger ahead of
    you,
  who will prepare your
    way;" Mark 1:2

just one more
    hour,
  please -
  let me enjoy the
  dreams of my
  wandering mind
   which leads me
   further from you;

just let me
            hit
    the snooze button
  and burrow under
  the blankets warm
  from my ambitions
      which lull me into
      that state of thinking
            i don't need
                    you;
just a couple of
              minutes
      to lie here
  and remember all the
  foolishness (so delicious
                  and filling)
  of yesterday,
        and daydream
        about all i might
          do today;
. . . but no,
  you come busting in,
        flipping on the lights,
        calling my name,
              dashing a bucket
              of grace into my
                      face,
    and while i splutter
              and mutter, you

    pull off the covers. hollering,
        "c'mon! a whole new
                  life
      is waiting for you!"

Thursday

For all this his anger has not
*   turned away;*
*   his hand is stretched out*
*   still. Isaiah 9:21b*

despite
  our clinging to
    burdensome grudges,

our apathy
      towards injustice,
   our doors slammed
      in refugee faces,
   our gluttony
      when it comes
      to creed,
you still reach
         out
to caress us
   with grace.

Friday

When John heard in prison what the Messiah was doing, he sent word by his disciples and said to him, "Are you the one who is to come, or are we to wait for another?" Matthew 11:2

we sit at the
   window waiting
 for the next
   new hope to appear,
while you
  raid our closets
    for the naked;
  empty our pantries
    for the feast offered
    to the hungry;
  setting up
    another free clinic
  opening the door wide
    for all the outsiders.

Saturday

*as it is written in the book of the words of the prophet Isaiah,
   "The voice of one crying out
      in the wilderness:
   'Prepare the way of the
      Lord,
   make his paths straight.'"* Luke 3:4

help us to prepare
by listening to
  that grumbling neighbor,

giving away more
to strangers
  than we will to
  family and friends,
waiting patiently
for grace,
  than rushing around
  to get all our lists
  marked off.

Fourth Week of Advent

December 18/Sunday

Praise him with clanging
    cymbals;
praise him with loud
    clashing cymbals! Psalm 150:5

the beep of
  the check-out
    scanner
 seems to play
 'he shall feed his
    flock'
as items for the
  food pantry
    pass by;
the rhythmic
  chiming of the bell,
 calling folks to
 place their offerings
in the red bucket
  which will
  overflow with
    hope
 for the homeless;
the broom swishing
  metronomically
 as the high schooler
 moves down the
    walk, brushing
  off the sand
  blown about by
  the early morning
    breeze:

everything,
    every thing
  praises God!

December 19/Monday

On that day the Lord will extend his hand yet a second time to recover the remnant that is left of his people, from Assyria, from Egypt, from Pathros, from Ethiopia, from Elam, from Shinar, from Hamath, and from the coastlands of the sea. Isaiah 11:11

we are hard at
       work,
   passing bills,
   raising money,
     building walls and
         fences,
 while you are
        busy
   digging tunnels
   under all our
       prejudices;
we put up more
    and more
  lighthouses to warn
   ships with
   banned cargo
    to beware,
      and you
  are bent over
  the oars, silently
    rowing your
    precious
   to safe harbor;
on that day,
    bring us -
the fearful,
    and the faithful,
the outraged
    and the hopeful,
the favorites
    and the outcast -

home.

December 20/Tuesday

Sing to him a new song;
  play skillfully on the
    strings, with loud
    shouts. Psalm 33:13

the little girl
  sitting on the
  shaky stool, plinking
    the keys of
    the out-of-tune
      cracked piano
in the corner of
  the shelter;
the teen-age
  group
acapellaing *O Holy Night*
into a hip-hop
      version
  with the beat box
  provided by the
    old vet in
    the wheelchair
  on his front porch;
the silent
    yearnings
  of a soldier
    providing a
    counterpoint
  to the call to
      prayer
  from the minaret;
new songs are
  all around us,
  are we listening?

December 21/Wednesday

But she was much perplexed by his words and pondered what sort of greeting this might be. Luke 1:29

really?

no running down the
      hall, screaming,

'Mama! Mama!'
no falling over
            gobsmacked;
no looking around
      for your friends
      to jump out of their
              hiding places,
   shouting, 'got you!'
no stunned silence,
      hard over the mouth,
      not knowing what to say;
just
      "much perplexed"?
so calm
        collected
      aware
however did
   you do it?

December 22/Thursday

Its gates will never be shut by day--and there will be no night there.
Revelation 21:25

at the front desk,
     Pete is overwhelmed
     by the number of
            folks
       insisting they have
       guaranteed reservations
         for the
                suites
         on the top floors;
a crowd is clustered
around the concierge
            desk,
   trying to get Mike's
              attention (with
      at east $50 folded in
                  their palms)
        to get tickets
        for the streetcar which
        will take us down
        the see-through gold
                streets;

we are double-checking
   the floor plans at the
         website, trying to
         figure out exactly
            where
      we will place the
      antiques stored back
            home;
meanwhile,
         you
   and the maintenance
   crew are busy removing
         all
      the bars and locks
      from the gates, pouring
         so much water
         on the hinges, that
      when they rust, no
         human efforts will
         ever swing them
            shut;
then,
      wiping your hands
      on the bandana pulled
         out of your
         back pocket,
      you smile to yourself,
   'there. now no one can be
            turned
            away.'

December 23/Friday

For the LORD is our judge,
   the LORD is our ruler,
the LORD is our king;
   he will save us. Isaiah 33:22

our teacher,
   you guide our hands
         under the lines
         of words, as
      we learn of your grace
      to sing your praise;
our companion,
   you refuse to walk

                        on, when
            we fall behind
                        or
        to let go of
                        our hands
            when we stand
            at the edge
                        of the abyss;
our voice coach,
    you stretch our
                        range,
        enabling us to
            project to
            the very far reaches
                of power,
    on behalf of those
        who are always
                        silenced;
our sister,
    our brother,
    our friend,
        our hope,
our all.

December 24/Saturday

*"to give light to those who sit
    in darkness and in the
    shadow of death,
  to guide our feet into the
    way of peace."* Luke 1:79

overnight,
heavy and wet,
covering the walks and streets,
temptations fall quietly
drifting up to our doors
and window sashes,
yet very early, you are
up
shoveling and clearing
the road for us;
the indifference
of our hearts
seeps out,

glazing our relationships
even with (no, especially)
those we don't know
with that permanentfrost
that causes us to slip
and slide through life,
until your tears' saltiness
melts the thickest layer
of ice imaginable;

as you prepare that
pathway
for us
to your kingdom,
illuminate it with your
grace,
so we will have no trouble
finding it.

Christmas Eve

*And he will come to Zion as
      Redeemer,* Isaiah 59:20a

when the grinchies
  would steal the season
  right from under us with
      their sad mournful
      songs about the
      state of the world,
  still
        Hope stands
      on the corner,
    her sweet soprano floating
      above the carolers
  in the silent night;

when the mongers of fear
  keep their stores open 24/7,
    rattling sabers in
      front of wide-eyed
      children,
    opening up their stockpiles
      of might so all may buy,
  still
        Peace wanders

        the world, its light
           piercing the shadows
          drawing all people closer
              together;

when despair stares
        us in the eye,
    daring us to find any
      reason to step outside
       of our worries
       and doubts,
  still
        Delight throws open
    the front door,
     grabs us by
     the hand,
  sits behind us on
    the sled
and wrapping his arms
tight around our waist,
   pushes off from the
      top of Zion Hill,
  singing, 'Joy to the
     world . . .'

Christmas Day

God's love was revealed to us in this way: God sent his only Son into the world so that we might live through him. 1 John 4:9

in the rustle of children
shaking presents,
in the hustle of kittens
scrambling up trees,
you stealthily tunnel
your way under the
flooring;

tossing all the traditional
marches in the shredder,
you collaborate
with the choir director,
composing a simple
oratorio for this night,
stressing that 'the tenors

are going to have to
reach that high note'

cup in hand,
you worm your way
through the office party,
touching us on the
shoulder,
subtly cracking the
combinations
of our frozen hearts,
to slip the still warm
loaves inside.

come,
Saboteur of our weary years,
bringing the Gift we need.

1st Sunday after Christmas

When Joseph awoke from sleep, he did as the angel of the Lord commanded him; Matthew 1:24a

when we
  long to believe
  Christmas is just a
     once-a-year dream,
point to the people who are
  searching through the
     ribbons and paper for
  grace;
  turning the empty
     boxes over, in case
     there is any
  hope
     stuck in the corners;
  walking the streets
     longing to hear the
  Babe
     calling their name.

December 26

*I treasure your word in my
       heart,* Psalm 119:11a

as we carefully
    wrap the crèche
    figurines in tissue paper,
  and place them in the
      box carried
    to the attic until next year,
take that Word
which seems so
  insignificant and
  outdated,
slipping it into our
  hearts, where
it will whisper to
      us
in the empty moments ahead.

December 27

Whoever has the Son has life; whoever does not have the Son of God does not have life. 1 John 5:12

    Bethlehem's
baby did not come
  so we could
  clean up his mess,
  hold his finger when he
      tried to walk,
  sing lullabies to put him
      asleep,
but so, he might
  change our lives,
  show us the way to
      grace, and
  cradle us in love.

December 28

*He who sits in the heavens
    laughs;* Psalm 2:4a

reading our weighty
  treatises on incarnation,
listening to our carefully
  crafted sermons
  and songs,

watching us try
  to fit the baby
  into the car seat
  so he has to go
  where we want,
you break into great guffaws,
wiping the tears
    from your eyes
    with a bandana,
laughing, 'you
don't have a clue
as to what is going
to happen, do you?'

December 29

On the last day of the festival, the great day, while Jesus was standing there, he cried out, "Let anyone who is thirsty come to me, and let the one who believes in me drink. As the scripture has said, 'Out of the believer's heart shall flow rivers of living water.'"
John 7:37-38

as we are determined
to store up the
    waters
  until they become vintage,
you take the
    tubing, bottles, caps
    out of our hands, shouting,
'you're just the fountain;
let them flow!'

December 30

It will be said on that day,
  Lo, this is our God; we
    have waited for him, so
    that he might save us. Isaiah 25:9a

potholes being filled
    in,
shelters closing
  because they are
  no longer needed,
the poor sitting
    on corporate boards,

these are the days
we know are ahead,
  because you have come.

December 31

Trust in the LORD forever,
  for in the LORD GOD
  you have an everlasting
    rock. Isaiah 26:4

when the thunder
of angry words rattles
  the windows;
when the strong wind
of pious platitudes
  howls through
  trees;
when sorrow lashes
  all around us,
we long for you,
and seek your light
 as the shadows
 creep up on us.

January 1

On the lips of children and of babes
  you have found praise . . . Psalm 8:2a *(The Grail)*

in early morning's
  'goo-goos,'
we hear your
 glory sung;

in evening's
  lullabies full
  of 'ba-bas,'
 we are cradled
in your
 grace.

2nd Sunday after Christmas

for all that is in the world – the desire of the flesh, the desire of the eyes, the pride in riches – comes not from the Father but from the world. 1 John 2:16

all our appetites
   unsatisfied;
focused on the
hot body paraded
  by the media;
told (by smiling preachers)
that prosperity is
    to be expected, we
may just miss
the bubbling laugh
  of a toddler,
the wheel chaired dancer
   on the stage;
the feast of
  brokenness and
  hope.

January 2

Now faith is the assurance of things hoped for, the conviction of things not seen. Hebrews 11:1

where we see
    a grocery list,
  you hope we
  will feed the
      hungry;
where we see
    a long weekend,
  you hope we
    will work on
    affordable housing;
where we see
   a scruffy sort
    with an outstretched
        hand,
  you hope we
    will embrace a
    long-lost relative.

January 3

Then Jacob woke from his sleep and said, "Surely the LORD is in this place – and I did not know it!" Genesis 28:16

in

the shelters crammed
  with storm survivors;
the alleys where
  the broken make
  a home out of cardboard;

the graveyard
  where we garden as
  we visit our beloved,
you are,
just waiting for
us to notice.

January 4

I am writing to you . . . because . . . 1 John 2:12

the word of hope
  tweeted in the wee hours
  to a lonely teen;

the email dashed off
  to the across-the-ocean
  friends just diagnosed
    with cancer;

the heart emojied
  to the one loved
    in silence;

the lifetime shared
  with children
  in a classroom . . .

you don't always
write in cursive.

January 5

"I hereby command you: Be strong and courageous; do not be frightened or dismayed, for the LORD your God is with you wherever you go." Joshua 1:9

let us leave
    fear
  behind, eating its
  bowl of curse and worry,
as we set out
  on each day,
    slipping our trembling
    hand into your
  calm one.

Eve of Epiphany

From the womb of the
    morning,
  like dew, your youth will
    come to you. Psalm 110:3b

as we wander
    aimlessly
  through the shadows
  of our lives, may
    your light of
      grace
appear, born
from the depths
  of your love.

Epiphany and following

January 6 *(Epiphany)*

Its gates will never be shut by day—and there will be no night there.
Revelation 21:25

no eternal shadow
    awaits us,
  but the light
  of love
    streaming
  from your heart's

gates, which
  never swing
shut.

The readings for the dated days after the Epiphany are used only until the following Saturday evening.

January 7

who turns the rock into a
      pool of water,
  the flint into a spring of
      water. Psalm 114:8

you form a
    baptismal font
  from our granite
    grudges, so that
from our flinty
    hearts can
  flow a
    torrent
of your
  grace.

January 8

And as for me, this is my covenant with them, says the LORD: my spirit that is upon you, and my words that I have put in your mouth, shall not depart out of your mouth, or out of the mouths of your children's children, says the LORD, from now on and forever.
Isaiah 59:21

of all the gifts,
    property,
  inheritance,
    power, we
might pass on
to our descendants,
  it is that
  simple word
    grace
that is priceless.

January 9

Now the man who had been healed did not know who it was, for Jesus had disappeared in the crowd that was there. John 5:13

the Samaritan
  who fixes the flat
  and drives off with a wave;
the person ahead
of the weary mother
at the checkout
  who pays for
  her groceries;
the teenager
who shovels
  our sidewalk while
  we are at a funeral:
you keep disappearing
before we can thank you,

Friend!

January 10

I held out my hands all day
    long
  to a rebellious people,
who walk in a way that is
    not good,
  following their own
    devices; Isaiah 65:2

instead of keeping
your hands in
    your pockets
  while we continue
  to run pell-mell
  through the fields
of foolishness, you
   reach,
     so we
  can grasp your
  life in
ours.

January 11

*He makes wars cease to the
    end of the earth;
  he breaks the bow, and
    shatters the spear;
  he burns the shields with
    fire.* Psalm 46:9

we would stockpile
   more and more weapons,
  while you would
  empty granaries
    for the poor;
we would continue
to discover new
   ways of death,
  while you continue
  to craft clothes
  of life for us.

January 12

*But this is the one to whom I
    will look,
  to the humble and contrite
    in spirit,
  who trembles at my word.* Isaiah 66:2b

terror
    fear
  debt
   doubt
  death can all
knock us down,
    but
if we reach
out our shaky hands
   to grasp your
    Word,
you will draw us
    into
  your embrace of
  hope and life.

Eve of Baptism of the Lord

More majestic than the
    the thunders of mighty
    waters,
more majestic than the
    waves of the sea,
majestic on high is the
    LORD! Psalm 93:4

more powerful
  than the floods
 of our doubts
 and worries is
the still pool
of your heart, where

  we are immersed
  in your
grace.

Baptism of the Lord (Sunday between Jan. 7 and 13 inclusive) and following

Baptism of the Lord

The LORD sits enthroned
    over the flood;
  the LORD sits enthroned as
    king forever. Psalm 29:10

you leave
   exaltation's seat
 to splash us
 with water,
until we are
   drenched
 with your
grace.

Monday

He destined us for adoption as his children through Jesus Christ, according to the good pleasure of his will, Ephesians 1:5

when we
    are orphaned
  by fear,
   prejudice,
  worry,
    and shame,
you carry us
into your
    heart, where
 we are held
 forever.

Tuesday

I have heard of your faith in the Lord Jesus and your love toward all the saints, Ephesians 1:15

in the songs
    of love
  to the folks
  in the nursing home;
in the calls
    for hungry children
  to gather around
  our tables;
in the whispers
    of hope
  offered to
    the despairing,
you hear the
  cacophony
of faith.

Wednesday

For I, the LORD your God,
  hold your right hand;
it is I who say to you, "Do
     not fear,
  I will help you." Isaiah 41:13

whenever
   the world
  clenches its
      fist,

shaking it in
   our
  face, you
gently caress
our hearts, whispering,
'pay no mind,
   I AM
   here.'

Thursday

When the poor and needy
   seek water,
   and there is none,
   and their tongue is
      parched with thirst,
I the LORD will answer them,
   I the God of Israel will not
      forsake them. Isaiah 41:17

mixing the
   salve
  from hope
   and grace,
you spread it
on lips cracked
   by grief
and tongues
  swollen by the
      blues, so
we may drink
deeply from your
  heart.

Friday

I am the LORD, I have called
   you in righteousness,
   I have taken you by the
      hand and kept you;
I have given you as a
      covenant to the
      people,
   a light to the nations, Isaiah 42:6

our calling:
not adulating applause,
    but giving
  attention to the poor;
not glory,
    but grace
    discovered
  in the grittiness
  of each day;
not pats on the back,
    but holding the hands
    of all the forgotten.

Saturday

I will sing to the LORD as
    long as I live;
  I will sing praise to my
    God while I have
    being. Psalm 104:33

with my last
    breath,
  may i sing
    your praise,
  as my voice
  joins the choir
gone on
    before me.

Week following Sunday between Jan. 14 and 20 inclusive

Sunday

I am about to do a new
    thing;
  now it springs forth, do
    you not perceive it?
I will make a way in the
    wilderness
  and rivers in the desert. Isaiah 43:19

we could sit
  in despair's
    desert,

    counting each
    grain of the grudges
    sticking to our life,
        or
    wash them
off with a quick
dip in the rivers
  of hope.

Monday

I have swept away your
    transgressions like a
    cloud,
  and your sins like mist;
return to me, for I have
    redeemed you. Isaiah 44:22

having hung up
the broom after
    sweeping away the litter
    of our lives, and
  freezing the mist
  of our mistakes
    to chill your drink,
you sit down
at the window,
watching,
  wondering,
    waiting . . .

. . . for the prodigals.

Tuesday

O LORD, you brought up my
    soul from Sheol,
  restored me to life from
    among those gone
    down to the Pit. Psalm 30:3

because
    you know
    the way out,
  we can take
  your hand, as

we follow the
crumbs of the broken
    bread
  into your grace.

Wednesday

For the sake of my servant
    Jacob,
  and Israel my chosen,
I call you by your name,
  I surname you, though you
    do not know me. Isaiah 45:4

whatever
    names
  the world
  may use,
remind us we
all bear the same
  spiritonym: **Beloved**

Thursday

And he said to them, "Pay attention to what you hear;" Mark 4:24a

listen to
  the songs of kids
  in the bathtub,
    not the shrill
    voices of haters;
  the wisdom of
  teenagers,
    not the immaturity
    of politicians;
  the whispers of
  hawks gliding above,
    not the braying
    of asinine anger.

Friday

And leaving the crowd behind, they took him with them in the boat, just as he was. Mark 4:36

we would like to
    clean you up, trim
  your beard and
    hair, wrap
  you in armanied
  array, a gold watch
    rolled on your wrist,
or
  we could get
as gritty with grace,
as dirty from
  walking the dusty
  roads of poverty,
as disheveled from
  wrestling with injustice

as you.

Saturday

even to your old age I am he,
   even when you turn gray I
     will carry you.
I have made, and I will bear,
   I will carry and will save. Isaiah 46:4

when others laugh
behind their hands,
  you still reach out
  to pat the head full
    of stress highlights;
when i do the
  old-man's-shuffle,
  you teach me new
    dance steps;
when i lie awake
  with memories
  tiptoeing through my head,
    you read me a sleepy story;
when I close
my eyes for the
last time, i awake
  in your embrace.

Week following Sunday between Jan. 21 and 27 inclusive

Sunday

You felt secure in your
*　　wickedness;*
*　you said, "No one sees*
*　　me."*
Your wisdom and your
*　　knowledge*
*　led you astray,*
and you said in your heart,
*　"I am, and there is no one*
*　　besides me."* Isaiah 47:10

when i am
　　anchored in
　anger;
　　locked in
　lust's embrace;
　　bound to
　bullying;
　　winning a game
　of grudges,
nobody really
notices, right?

except me
　(and thee)

Monday

for she said, "If I but touch his clothes, I will be made well."
Mark 5:28

sometimes,
　a thread of
　hope
　　might be all
　　we need
to weave new
　lives.

Tuesday

He ordered them to take nothing for their journey except a staff; no bread, no bag, no money in their belts; Mark 6:8

no fancy cars
    or
  large sanctuaries;
no entourage
    or
  governing board;
no barred robes
    or
  diamond-studded
      crosses . . .
just trust, that
we will find
  the places (and
  people) to serve.

Wednesday

saying to the prisoners,
      "Come out,"
  to those who are in
      darkness, "Show
      yourselves."
They shall feed along the
      ways,
  on all the bare heights
      shall be their pasture; Isaiah 49:9

you pick the
    lock of our
    hearts so we
  may walk unafraid;
you light
    candles
  in the side chapels
    of our souls;
you feed us
    under the bridges
  of heartache;
you gather us
    in the meadows
  rippling with hope.

Thursday

See, I have inscribed you on
      the palms of my hands. Isaiah 49:16a

etched on your
    hands,
  you remember us
  every time you
    wash your face,
  do the dishes,
bake bread,
  shape a star,
    write a sonnet,
cradle us.

Friday

Why was no one there when
    I came?
  Why did no one answer
    when I called? Isaiah 50:2a

too busy with
  games and searches
  on our devices, we
  never hear the
  doorbell;
plugged into the
    noises and distractions
    of the world, we
  do not hear your
    voice, and
slide further into
our loneliness.

Saturday

Therefore the law was our disciplinarian until Christ came, so that we might be justified by faith. Galatians 3:24

so engrossed with
making sure that we
  toe the
    line,
  keep our souls
    spotless,
  learn every jot
  and tittle of the
    rules,

before sending us
off to bed without a
    snack,
the babysitter
never notices
you
  sneaking into our
  rooms, and
with a shushing finger
to your lips,
  tiptoe us out
into the firefly-spackled
    evening
where we twirl and
twirl in circles until
collapsing in the dew,
watching the dawn
color the morning sky.

Week following Sunday between Jan. 28 and Feb. 3 inclusive, except when this Sunday is Transfiguration

Sunday

I, I am he who comforts you;
  why then are you afraid of
    a mere mortal who
    must die,
  a human being who fades
    like grass? Isaiah 51:12

we could let them
control our lives:
    the bully neighbor,
    the critical friend,
    the cold-shouldered lover,
    the dissembling politicians,
      or
  we can just crawl up
  into your comforting arms
and be rocked in
    your grace.

Monday

But when the fullness of time had come, God sent his Son, born of a woman, born under the law, Galatians 4:4

not when we
were wise, but
    foolish;
not when we
were wealthy, but
    broke;
not when we
were settled, but
    homeless,
  that
is when you
made us your own.

Tuesday

For you shall not go out in
    haste,
  and you shall not go in
    flight;
for the LORD will go before
    you,
  and the God of Israel will
    be your rear guard. Isaiah 52:12

when we let
    you
  take the lead,
we move slow
    enough
to see joy in
  mud-splattered dogs;
to hear the wonder
  in childish questions;
to taste grace
  in sweet corn;
to know love
  in the gaze
  of another.

Wednesday

And he sighed deeply in his spirit and said, "Why does this generation ask for a sign? Truly I tell you, no sign will be given to this generation." Mark 8:12

may we stop
asking for a sign
  of peace,
      hope,
    grace,
      gentleness,
and be the
life
that others are seeking.

Thursday

And he sternly ordered them not to tell anyone about him.   Mark 8:30

help us to
    stop flapping
   our mouths
  about you,
and spend more time
showing you
     with
our hearts
  our hands,
    our feet.

Friday

By contrast, the fruit of the Spirit is love, joy, peace, patience, kindness, generosity, faithfulness, gentleness, and self-control.
Galatians 5:22-23a

remind us
that the fruit
  are not the harvest
  which we gather,
but the seeds planted
deep within us, so
we may grow into
our life with the
     Spirit.

Saturday

*Thus says the LORD:
Maintain justice, do
  what is right,*

*for soon my salvation will
   come,
and my deliverance be
   revealed.* Isaiah 56:1

while we are waiting
to drive down streets of gold,
   move into our mansions
   and take harp lessons,
let us sing songs of hope
   to the lonely,
   repair homes for seniors,
   fill in the potholes, and
give bus passes to the poor.

Week following Sun. between Feb. 4 and 10 inclusive, except when this Sunday is Transfiguration

Sunday

Therefore, since we are surrounded by so great a cloud of witnesses, Hebrews 12:1a

open our eyes
to the witnesses
around us:
   the poor who look
      after those in need;
   the broken who offer
      healing to their neighbors;
   the young dog walker
      who stops to share
      joy with each
      person she meets.

Monday

But they did not understand what he was saying and were afraid to ask him. Mark 9:32

why is t whenever you say,
   'love your enemy;
   feed the hungry;
   welcome the outsiders;
   let go of your grip

        on your resumes;
    forgive (every) one
       (every) time'
we hear just the opposite?

Tuesday

Is it not to share your bread
       with the hungry,
  and bring the homeless
      poor into your house;
when you see the naked, to
      cover them,
  and not to hide yourself
      from your own kin? Isaiah 58:7

we don't mind
offering the Table's pieces
   of bread to those
   around us, but
  our homes,
    our pantries,
      our clothes,

our selves?

Wednesday

See, the LORD's hand is
  not too short to save,
nor his ear too dull to hear. Isaiah 59:1

if we would
just stop knocking
    your hands away,
  others would be helped;
if we would just
stop babbling all our
bromides and braggadocios,
    you could hear the
  pain of our hearts.

Thursday

Lift up your eyes and look
      around;

they all gather together,
 they come to you;
your songs shall come from
 far away,
 and your daughters shall
 be carried on their
 nurses' arms. Isaiah 60:4

it is precisely the ones
we worry about:
 the other-religioned outsiders,
 the tattooed and pierced
  knot of kids,
 the ex-cons looking for a job,
 the family on the street that
you send to turn us
from gloomy grumps into
 angels of wonder and hope.

Friday

to proclaim the year of the
 LORD's favor,
 and the day of vengeance
 of our God;
 to comfort all who mourn; Isaiah 61:2

let this day
 be the one of peace;
may this week
 be the one of hope;
may this month
 be the one of justice;
may this year
 be the one of grace;

may this be so.

Saturday

proclaim the message; be persistent whether the time is favorable or unfavorable; convince, rebuke, and encourage, with the utmost patience in teaching. 2 Timothy 4:2

may we never
stop speaking words of hope;

may we be dogged
in our commitment to peace;

may we always
be patient when you
do not do things our way.

Week following Sun. between Feb. 11 and 17 inclusive, except when this Sunday is Transfiguration

Sunday

Again Jesus spoke to them, saying, "I am the light of the world. Whoever follows me will never walk in darkness but will have the light of life." John 8:12

in the dim recesses
    of our fears,
  a candle flickers
  in the distance,
  gradually drawing
    closer,
until we see you
walking toward us,
  and, taking us
  by the hand, you
lead us into life.

Monday

*They rise in the darkness as
    a light for the upright;
  they are gracious,
    merciful, and
    righteous. Psalm 112:4*

we long to stay
  in bed, cozy
  and warm
  under the covers
    of our apathy
    and doubts, but

you splash
cold water in our faces,
   throwing clothes at us,
inviting us to join you in
   feeding the hungry,
     sheltering the poor,
   warming the cold
   who are standing out
   in the predawn shadows.

Tuesday

In all their distress
  he was distressed;
the angel of his presence
  saved them. Isaiah 63:9a (alt. reading)

you do not stand
   off at a
   distance, cold
  and indifferent to
   our disappointments
   and griefs, but
you gather them to
your heart, where
  they break it
  over and over
again.

Wednesday

Yet, O LORD, you are our
    Father;
  we are the clay, and you
    are our potter;
  we are the work of your
    hand. Isaiah 64:8

but now,
   with our arrogance
   gripped tightly in our
     hands,
  standing knee deep
   in our foolish deeds,
  dressed in the rags

    made out of our
        poor choices,
you take us by
        the heart,
   transforming us into
the children of your
        hopes.

Thursday

I was ready to be sought
       out by those who did
       not ask,
  to be found by those who
       did not seek me.
I said, "Here I am, here I
       am."
  to a nation that did not call
       on my name.   Isaiah 65:1

no matter how
    stubborn
  we are, you
    are flexible;
however often we
    refuse to say
    your name, you
  whisper ours;
wherever we long
to flee from you,
    you are waiting
       for us, just
  around the corner
  with your hope.

Friday

But be glad and rejoice
      forever
  in what I am creating;
for I am about to create
      Jerusalem as a joy,
  and its people as a delight. Isaiah 65:18

where we see
    rotting neighborhoods,
  you envision
    communities of hope;
where we hear
    the echoes of
    empty concrete canyons,
  you listen to the
    laughter of children
    in the playgrounds;
as we wander down
    streets littered
    with despair, we
  find you picking
  up lives and creating
     joy in broken hearts.

Saturday

but if we have food and clothing, we will be content with these.
1 Timothy 6:8

typically, we
can only wear
  1 shirt,
  pair of pants,
  shoes, etc.,
at a time,

so
why are we
always hungry for
more?

Week following Sun. between Feb 18 and 24 inclusive, except when this Sunday is Transfiguration

Sunday

As a mother comforts her
    child,
  so I will comfort you;
  you shall be comforted in
    Jerusalem. Isaiah 66:13

into neighborhoods
    crumbling in despair,
  you come, wearing your tool belt
    filled with hope and grace;

where families are torn apart
    by old grudges
    and fresh wounds,
  you swaddle them in
  cloths drenched with
    peace and forgiveness;

in places where children
are abandoned on the streets
    by politicians and platitudes,
  you gather them up
    and bring them home with you.

Monday

"Blessed are the poor in spirit, for theirs is the kingdom of heaven."
Matthew 5:3

blessed are the
    poor who
  dare to share
  their spirit of
    hope
even when all
the odds
  are stacked against
    them.

Tuesday

"Do not think that I have come to abolish the law or the prophets; I have come not to abolish but to fulfill." Matthew 5:17

you fulfill the
    law
  by standing in the
    dock in our place;
you fulfill the
    prophets
  by bringing us
  out of our exile;

you fulfill our
      hopes
  by becoming our
    life.

Wednesday

You will not fear the terror
    of the night,
  or the arrow that flies by
    day,
or the pestilence that stalks
    in darkness,
  or the destruction that
    wastes at noonday. Psalm 91:5-6

not the worries
    tip-toeing outside
    our souls,
nor the hurts
    thrown at us
    by our friends;
not the pandemic
    of terror flu,
nor those who
    would throw us
    under the street sweeper,

will ever make us
  afraid.

Thursday

Since, then, we have such a hope, we act with great boldness,
2 Corinthians 3:12

since we hope
    in your grace,
  we can be
    kinder;

since we hope
    in your blessings,
  we can be
    more generous;

since we hope
> in your acceptance,
> we can become
>> more just.

Friday

But we have this treasure in clay jars, so that it may be made clear that this extraordinary power belongs to God and does not come from us. 2 Corinthians 4:7

> not fine bone china,
>> or centuries old vases;
> not heirloom jewelry in a vault,
>> or antique furniture collecting dust;
> but clay,
>> dust of the earth,
> cradled and shaped
> by your hands
>> of love,
> simply
> for weakness,
>> service,
>> kindness,
> hope.

Saturday

"Beware of practicing your piety before others in order to be seen by them; for then you have no reward from your Father in heaven."
Matthew 6:1

> tempted to pat
>> ourselves on the
> soul
>> for how spiritual we are,
>>> perhaps
> we need to look
> in the closet
>> until we find
>> the work clothes
> you have made
>> just for us.

Week following Sun. Feb 25 and 29 inclusive, except when this Sunday is Transfiguration

Sunday

"You always have the poor with you, but you do not always have me." John 12:8

maybe
    the poor are
    always with us
  because
we focus more on
      'us'
than on them.

Monday

"When you are praying, do not heap up empty phrases as the Gentiles do; for they think that they will be heard because of their many words." Matthew 6:7

instead
    of platitudes
    and pious piles
  of words, let
us offer our empty
      hearts,

  so you may fill
  them with yourself.

Tuesday

"For where your treasure is, there your heart will be also." Matthew 6:21

may we find our hearts,
  not in crammed
     closets or
    overflowing pantries;

 nor in shinier
     cars or
    biggie-sized homes,
      but in your

hope.

Wednesday

Because the LORD your God is a merciful God, he will neither abandon you nor destroy you; he will not forget the covenant with your ancestors that he swore to them. Deuteronomy 4:31

when we long
to walk away,
    you trail behind,
  refusing to take the hint;
when we offer you the
worst of our souls, you
    continue to give us
    the best of your
heart.

Thursday

"Do not judge, so that you may not be judged." Matthew 7:1

judgment tastes
    so delicious, until
  it is put on our
    plate;
punishment seems
    oh so right, until
  we are in the dock.

Friday

We are speaking in Christ before God. Everything we do, beloved, is for the sake of building you up. 2 Corinthians 12:19b

why do we find
    it so much easier
to kick the legs
out from under others,
    rather than offering
    our shoulder for
  support?

Saturday

*Lord, you have been our
    dwelling place
  in all generations.* Psalm 90:1

wherever –
   in alleys shadowed
      in poverty;
   in hospital rooms
      reeking of fear;
   in graveyards
      empty of laughter;
   in shelters
      overflowing with pain,

you are
   our home.

Transfiguration (Sunday preceding Lent) and following

Sunday

You yourselves are our letter, written on our hearts, to be known and read by all; 2 Corinthians 3:2

not a robo
      rejection letter,
   or spam;
not an anonymous
      complaint
   or a scam to
      bilk others,
but words of
         hope,
      grace,
      joy,
   and wonder –

that's what the Spirit
writes through us.

Monday

You shall love the LORD your God with all your heart, and with all your soul, and with all your might. Deuteronomy 6:5

i will whole-heartedly
   give into my lusts;
   gladly surrender my
      soul to my fears;

      strong-arm others
         out of my way with
         unrestrained joy,
and
grudgingly
offer you the
         leftovers of me.

Tuesday

These things I remember,
   as I pour out my soul:
how I went with the throng,
   and led them in procession
      to the house of God,
with glad shouts and songs
      of thanksgiving,
a multitude keeping
   festival. Psalm 42:4

it seems like only
       yesterday
 they fit so
   comfortably
 in our palms, as
 we paraded around the
    sanctuary
singing our glad songs (the
   teachers whispering,
   'they are not those kind
   of cymbals' when we tried
   to bang them together)
and bringing them up to the
      front to place
   on the Table;
now, hushed and still,
    we watch
   as a flame curls around the
    dry, crunchy, dusty
    leaves, crumbled up in
    an old pot,
 slowly reduced to ashes
      we will put on (not
    understanding why,
       perhaps)
    tomorrow

      and wear until the day
        our smudged lives
          are cleansed
          by the holy oil
          of your

tears.

Ash Wednesday

When the news reached the king of Ninevah, he rose from his throne, removed his robe, covered himself with sackcloth, and sat in ashes. Jonah 3:6

as the rest of
the slim crowd
moves towards the
exit,
i
slip into the
restroom, hoping
no one will follow;
i stand before
the mirror,
slowly shaking
my head at
the ashed
face staring
back at me;
as I turn on the
water
and reach for
a towel to scrub
it off,
you gently
touch my
hand, whispering,
'leave it on,
just for a little
while,
so folks will know
whose
you are.'
then,
you slip out the door,

hoping i
might
follow.

Thursday

He will regard the prayer of the
         destitute,
   and will not despise their
         prayer. Psalm 102:17

we look at
     the shaky,
     unshaven fellow
          holding the sign
          by the side of the road
          asking for $$$
     and discern a failure,

  but you see
    that prodigal
    who left home
    so long ago, and
      you begin to
      hand-write the
      party invitations;

just outside
the doors of the
         sanctuary,
  we impatiently
  listen to the 'sob
    story' we have heard
    a hundred times, slowly
         edging away (while
         stealing glances
         at our watch),

  but you take
  her by the hand,
      leading her over
      to the shady bench,
    sitting down and
    giving her your full
         attention, inviting
    "tell me more."

Friday

*Praise the LORD from the
 earth,
 you sea monsters and all
 deeps,
fire and hail, snow and frost,
 stormy wind fulfilling his
 command! Psalm 148:7-8*

though
　the snow piles up
　　　past
　　my second-story
　　　　windows;
though
　the winds chill
　　my soul until
　the temperature
　cannot be
　　　recorded;
though
　the rains rush
　　through my life
　washing away all
　my hopes and dreams;
though
　the monsters
　of my fitful sleep
　　　breach
　　the surface
　of my
　　　peace;
still, i
will praise
　　you.

Saturday

to speak evil of no one, to avoid quarreling, to be gentle, and to show every courtesy to everyone. Titus 3:2

we could
　　sit down on the
　　　　job,

refusing to speak
against injustice,
    or we can
    take a stand
 to lift others
 to their feet;
we could
  tighten our jaws
  and grind out bile
    towards others,
     or we can
     let our words
    be as gentle
    as a breeze;
we could
  slam the door
  in the face of
all whom we
    despise,
   or we can
   open our hearts
  and invite them in;
we could
  grab a thesaurus
  to find the weapons
    we need to win,
   or we can
   wrap our adversary
 in a hug of
    peace;
we could
  watch the
  immigrant struggling
    with her groceries
    in the pouring rain,
   or we can hold our
   umbrella over her
    while she unlocks
    the car door . . .
when we could be
what we have always
    been,
remind us
 who
 we might
    become.

1st Week of Lent

Sunday

For God's foolishness is wiser than human wisdom, and God's weakness is stronger than human strength. 1st Corinthians 1:25

gazing in the mirror,
you scoop up a gob
of greasepaint,
smearing it all over
your face,
adding the candy-red
gumdrop nose,
dabbing mauve stars,
mustard moons,
and iridescent comets
on your cheeks;
you pull on
the polka dotted suit,
the baggy sleeves
stuffed with grace;
sticking the seltzer bottle
filled with living water
in your back pocket;
you pull on your
three-times-too-big
scuffed shoes
and squeeze uncomfortably
into the kiddie car
disguised as a
firetruck;
waving and honking
the big-bulbed horn
you drive through
our lives,
calling out:
'wanna see Jesus?
. . . follow me!'

Monday

Do not say to yourself, "My power and the might of my own hand have gotten me this wealth." Deuteronomy 8:17

not the tasks
  i turn my
    hand to,
but the
  open palm
  of friendship
    i offer to
    another;
not a bigger
    house
  than my
    rival,
but the
  space i offer
     you
    in my soul;

not the wad
    of paper $$
   in my purse,
but the picture
  of the child
  i am mentoring;
not the toned
    muscles gained
   at the gym,
but the
  vulnerability
   i offer to
    my partner;

not the
  diploma on
  my wall,
but those
    words
  you write
  on my
    heart:
these are
    the true
  wealth
of my
   life.

Tuesday

The friendship of the LORD is
for those who fear him,
and he makes his covenant
known to them. Psalm 25:14

on a hot summer's
 day,
 the wind in our
 faces,
 salt tangy on
 our lips,
 you laugh with
 delight as
 you place my
 hand
 on the tiller, saying,
 "it's your turn; remember
 what i showed you."
on a cold winter
 morning, when
 it seems that
 the chill just won't
 let go of
 my heart,
 you pour me
 a strong cuppa,
 slathering butter
 and jam
 on just-baked
 bread, pushing it
 across the table to
 me;
as i wonder about
 the next step
 in this journey,
 worried what
 it might mean,
 you remind me,
 'sure, put me down
 as a reference; but
 you don't have
 to ask every
 time -

that's what
     friends
  are for."

Wednesday

"The wind blows where it chooses, and you hear the sound of it, but you do not know where it comes from or where it goes. So it is with everyone who is born of the Spirit." John 3:8

it is that
     breath
  which barely stirs
  the curtains
  on a steamy,
        summer night,
    yet
       cools our
       sweaty souls;
it can come
as a
     gust   strong enough

   to knock us
   off our feet,
  so we look around
     and see that
     mis
        s
         t
          e
           p
  we were about
     to take;
it is the
     aroma
  of bread
  fresh out of
     the oven,
   so yeasty
   and warm
  tickling our
  senses until
      we
  realize we are
     home,

    where you
    have been
        waiting.
for
    us.

Thursday

"Come," my heart says,
    "seek his face!"
Your face, LORD, do I seek. Psalm 27:8

i seek your
    face
  in every smooth-skinned,
  toned and tanned
      celebrity parading
      down the red carpet,
 not noticing your
    bright eyes watching
    me from the nest
        of crows' feet
    in the well-worn
    visage of the
        bag lady on
        the park bench;
i beat the bushes
    looking for you,
    counting to 100
 as slowly as i can,
    staying as close
    to home base
      as possible,
  while you prance
    beside me, your
    tail wagging in
  delight at being
  able to play with
 me;
i leave no stone
      unturned,
  determined to
  find the treasure
  promised on
  the faded map,

    until i turn around
      and find you
      planting a garden
          of joy
       in the rich soil
       disturbed by my
    anxiety.

Friday

He is your praise; he is your God, who has done for you these great and awesome things that your own eyes have seen.
Deuteronomy 10:21

so simple:
the sun
     which never
     sleeps in late
  or takes a sick
          day;
the spouse who,
      after 60 years,
     still sees the
     22-year-old face
      when he looks
      at his wife;
the trees,
     whose barren,
     brittle branches
  let Spring
          hibernate
  deep within;
the auroral zone
     which warms
     us on bitter
     winter nights
         with shimmering
         displays;
so ordinary,
we forget how
  awesome these
           things
   are, and so
we forget our

Praise.

Saturday

The woman said to him, "I know that Messiah is coming" (who is called Christ). "When he comes, he will proclaim all things to us."
John 4:25

to those
    bullied
  in schoolyards,
      you proclaim
      friendship;
to those
    ostracized
  because they
  are 'different,'
      you proclaim
      acceptance;
to those
    refugees
  who should go
  back to where
  they came from,
      you proclaim
      welcome;

to us
    who see
    people only as
  'those,'
      you proclaim
      mercy.

2nd **Week in Lent**

Sunday

Then the LORD put out his hand and touched my mouth; and the LORD said to me,
    "Now I have put my words
        in your mouth. . . " Jeremiah 1:9

they
  can become the
      punctum
    of animosity,

             or the healing balm
             for the sores
                    on another's
                         soul;
they
   can be the
             bricks
          in a wall which
          separates us,
       or the bridge
       over the canyon
             of our prejudices;
they
   can burn the
             dreams
          of our friends
          to ashes,
       or rekindle the
       dying embers
             of their hope;
so
   give us the
          words we
          need, especially
yours.

   (*punctum* is sometimes used to describe a 'flash point')

Monday

I lift up my eyes to the
      hills--
   from where will my help
      come? Psalm 121:1

you shaped the
          stars,
      yet thought
      to put a
          twinkle
   in our
      eyes;

you carved
          rivers
       through canyons,

    and gave us
        tears to
        share with
            laughter;

you shattered
          moons
    into asteroids,
  and put
        hearts
      deep within
  us which break
    for others;

you ignited that
          spark
    which flung
     universes
  into space, yet
    effortlessly
      take a
     moment to
      help us.

Tuesday

I remember the devotion of your
        youth,
    your love as a bride,
how you followed me in the
        wilderness,
   in a land not sown. Jeremiah 2:2

i remember when
       i was a little
           child,
  clinging so tightly
  to you,
      determined never,
      ever to let go, for
        fear of losing you;

i remember those
    promises
  i made, holding hands

                    with you, looking
                  you in the eyes
                  with a passion
               which seemed to
               dim the full moon
                        shining through
                        the window;

i remember following
          you with unfettered
                   enthusiasm,
          carefully placing my
          feet in the impressions
                   you left
               in my heart,
          convinced you knew
          a path i could not see;

i remember
          and wonder
why
          did i

forget?

Wednesday

When Jesus saw him lying there and knew that he had been there a long time, he said to him, "Do you want to be made well?" John 5:6

the grudge weighting
          for decades
          and slowly bending
                   my back
          until my forehead
          almost scrapes the
                   ground?
the canker sores
          on the inside

          of my mouth
          caused by chewing
                   on the acidic
                            words
          i have flung at
                   others?

the blisters
    on my feet
  from running too
      fast
    and far too
      long
  trying to get
    away from
      you?
made well?
  dare i?

Thursday

*"For my people are foolish,
  they do not know me;
they are stupid children,
  they have no
    understanding.
They are skilled in doing
    evil,
  but do not know how to do
    good."* Jeremiah 4:22

lifelong learners
    of vileness,
  we are constantly
    checking out
    the latest videos
      and DIY books;

skilled in the
    rhetoric of
    bullying, we take
      every advantage
      offered by the
      social media;

we proudly
    hang the
    framed PhDs
      in iniquity
  obtained from the
  diploma mills
    accessed online;

so
>   send us back
>   to your
>   kindergarten
>   where we can
>   begin to learn
>   anew the ABCs of
>   kindness,
>   justice,
>   and grace.

Friday

Run to and fro through the
*   streets of Jerusalem,*
* look around and take note!*
Search its squares and see
* if you can find one person*
who acts justly
* and seeks truth—*
so that I may pardon
*   Jerusalem.* Jeremiah 5:1

we chased after
        the politicians,
    for surely they
        have our best
        interests at heart,
                only to find
                them lining
            their pockets;
we rushed to fill
    the classrooms
    of the philosophers,
    convinced they
            knew the answers
            to the questions
        burdening so many,
    but they were
    simply passing out
            copies of last
            term's syllabus;
we wandered
down back alleys,
    listening to the
    whispers of

      those standing in
      shadowed
          doorways,
       promising that
       their deal was
          fair and square,
   but it turned out
   we were only buying
       fools' gold.

now
   what do we
 do?

Saturday

Be strong, and let your heart
      take courage,
all you who wait for the
      LORD. Psalm 31:24

when cancer
     weakens
   our resolve,
when cracks
    appear in
   our hearts,
when sorrow
    absorbs
   every tear
  we have -
let us
stand up
 to these
bullies and
  not let them
  push us around;
when the shadows
    seep under
   the edges of
     our doors,
 slowly creeping
towards our bed,
  ready to grab
  us by the hand

        and drag us
          into our fears,
let us wait,
  for the Lord has
    just gone down
      the hall to get us
      a glass of water
and will be back
  to sit by our
    side until
morning.

3rd *Week of Lent*

Sunday

"All things are lawful for me," but not all things are beneficial. "All things are lawful for me," but I will not be dominated by anything.
1 Corinthians 6:12

when anger
     longs to
    lead me around
    by the nose,
let me smell the
warm, yeasty
     aroma of
      your grace;
when judgment
     wants to have
     the upper hand,
let me walk
in the faltering
      footsteps
    of my foolish
    friends;
when i am
    convinced i
    should be the
concertmaster
  in the kingdom's
    symphony,
    let me gladly
    take the last seat
    in the row
    of piccolos;

when my desires
      want to run
     this show called
        life,
let me simply
step aside so
     you can
      show me the
path.

Monday

"Stand in the gate of the LORD's house, and proclaim there this word, and say, Hear the word of the LORD, all you people of Judah, you that enter these gates to worship the LORD. Jeremiah 7:2

let us stand
   on the shop floor
   and declare,
 'let this be the
     place where
     each person
     is paid fairly;'
let us stand
   in the emergency room
   and say aloud,
 'let this be the
     place where
     people get the
     medical care
   they not only need,
      but deserve;'
let us stand
   in the class rooms
    and make known,
 'let this be the
     place where
     children will
     receive a first-class
      education,
   no matter their
   status in society;'
let us stand
   in every place,
   next to every person,

with you, Lord,
let us stand.

Tuesday

As the scripture has said, 'Out of the believer's heart shall flow rivers of living water.'" John 7:38

when we are
    tempted
  to brick up our
    hearts
 to dam off
 the overflow;
when we
    turn
  the faucets
  tighter and tighter
     until
 only a drip
 every hour or
      so
  appears;
when we
    call in the
    plumber to
     reconfigure
    the pipes
 so it runs
 round and round
   like a circulating
  fountain;
when we
   fill up our
   bathtubs
  and every bucket
  we have because
    of a rumored
    hazardous
 spill,
remind us
of the others
  who are as
    thirsty
 as we once
 were.

Wednesday

Why then has this people
    turned away
  in perpetual backsliding?
They have held fast to
    deceit,
  they have refused to
    return. Jeremiah 8:5b

like kids on
  snow-covered
  Mistake Hill, we
sit down on our
    sleds, and swoosh
    down to the bottom
  as quickly as we can,
and, then drag them up
  to the top to
    repeat our
    foolishness
  over and over;
we grasp
  the lies we tell
    ourselves,
  clutching them so
    tightly until
    they become
  imprinted on
  the walls of
    our souls;
we sweep you
into our arms,
    twirling around
    the floor to
  seduction's sweet
    strains, our
  clumsy feet clad
  in the too-tight
  sin-cobbled shoes
  constantly crushing
    your toes
    and dreams for us,
and when the band

stops, we
smile and whisper
in your ear,

'let's do it again!'

Thursday

One thing I asked of the
LORD,
 that will I seek after:
to live in the house of the
LORD
 all the days of my life,
to behold the beauty of the
LORD,
 and to inquire in his
  temple. *Psalm 27:4*

walking in the
 fog, hoping
 i will not
  stumble
 along the way . . .
lying in the
 brightness
 of the full
  moon
 shining through
 the bedroom window . . .
watching the
 mist slowly
 drift along
 the curving
  surface
 of the river . . .
turning over the
 soil,
 preparing it to
 welcome the
  seeds
 brooding with
  lettuce,
  tomatoes,
  flowers,
  carrots . . .

sitting in the
    silence
 of the backyard,
  as my thoughts
  slowly
    drift
  towards you . . .
. . . i find myself
    finally
  at home.

Friday

Do you not know that all of us who have been baptized into Christ Jesus were baptized into his death? Romans 6:3

baptized
    with you,
 we swim in the
 warm waters of
    joy, racing
  you to see
  who gets to
    the far shore
  first;
buried
    with you,
  we are planted
  in grace's rich
    soil,
    nourished by
    the Spirit so
  we might stretch
  towards glory's
    morning;
united
    with you,
  we hold hands
  with the rest
    of your siblings,
 crossing death's
 busy road
    into the
  kingdom.

Saturday

Teach me to do your will,
   for you are my God.
Let your good spirit lead me
   on a level path. Psalm 143:10

i could
  tail temptation
      down the
      blind alleys
   of its
       maze;
i could
   follow the
  pride piper
     until
    caught in
    that trap
   i would never
      escape;
i could
   let death
   coach me
  on every
    wrinkle
  in its
   playbook;
or
  i could let
     you
    guide me
     into grace.

4th Week in Lent

Sunday

And he cautioned them, saying, "Watch out -- beware of the yeast of the Pharisees and the yeast of Herod." Mark 8:15

may the warmth
   of your living waters
   be just
  what those the

world leaves out
    in the cold
  need;
may the saltiness
  of your tears
 bring
 healing to
   the wounds
   of those
  pierced by
    hatred;
may the gentleness
  of your touch
 knead the sore
   muscles
   of those whose
  backs are
  stiffened by
  12-hour shifts
  in oncology
    units;
may the yeast
  of your justice
 enable us
 to rise and
  feed the
  hungry outcasts

 all around us.

Monday

"There is a boy here who has five barley loaves and two fish. But what are they among so many people?" John 6:9

the half-empty
   bottle
  of water
 we toss into
 the waste can
   at work;
the ends
  of the
  bread
 we let turn

    moldy in
        the fridge;
the veggies
      we leave
    on our plate
    at the restaurant,
  so we have room
  for dessert;
the compassion
      we toss
    into the coin
    jar on top
    of our dresser
  at the end
  of the day:
our simple gifts
    could make
    such a feast
of
      hope,
    healing, and
    grace
  for others if
we would only
put them in your
      hands.

Tuesday

But if you listen to me, says the LORD, and bring in no burden by the gates of this city on the sabbath day, but keep the sabbath day holy and do no work on it, Jeremiah 17:24

may this day
    be less running
        around
      with errands, and
        more
  walking with you;
may this day
    offer less talking
        and
      more silence;
may this day
    be less about
        accumulating

    and more about
        giving (away);
may this day
   contain less
          grumbling
  and more
        songs
 to you;
may this day
  be less focused
        on me, and
  more on the ones i
     love (especially
   you);
may this day
  be less about
      doing, and
  more about
    being;

may this day
    be sabbath.

Wednesday

The vessel he was making of clay was spoiled in the potter's hand, and he reworked it into another vessel, as seemed good to him.
Jeremiah 18:4

the fingers
  that unfolded
  butterflies' wings
 and waved goodbye
to them
    now smooth
    the wrinkles
 of our souls;

those hands
  callused by
  shaping craggy
     mountains
  now gently
  caress us into
     being;

that breath
   which melted
       glaciers
     into blue-green
       oceans
now fills
our lungs
   with life
as you
  craft us
 into earthenware
    vessels
   to hold
   the dreams
of others.

Thursday

We know that the whole creation has been groaning in labor pains until now; Romans 8:22

resistant
    to directions,
 we are pretty
    sure
 we don't need
to be shown the
   way out
  of our shadows;
we tap our
   pencil
 against our
  teeth, eager
  for the test
to be over so
   we can
   get to the
  fun part
  of life;
groaning
   under our breath,
 nervously drumming
 our fingers on the
    wheel, we
  try to change
  the signal by

    sheer
        concentration;
give us
    the
patience
  to wait for
  your hope
    to come,
just around the
      corner
of our faith.

Friday

*I will tell of your name to my
    brothers and sisters;
 in the midst of the
    congregation I will
    praise you:* Psalm 22:22

all the parties
   i no longer
 get invited to,
all the kids
   standing in front
   of their lockers
 snickering at me;

all the teachers who whisper,
   'he had such potential,
  what happened?'
it's as if i have
 a 'kick me'
      sign

   on my back;
if i mention
    your name,
 people fall down
    laughing;

if i don't,
 another hole
 burns in my soul;

like fawkes,
    i dissolve
  into ashes, yet
    come back
    again and again;
your words
keep spilling
    out of my
      mouth,
  no matter
  how hard i try
    to put padlocks
and chains
    around them.

Saturday

Simon Peter answered him, "Lord, to whom can we go? You have the words of eternal life." John 6:68

word of life
come to us,
so we may hear
your call,
then let us
go with you
to the death
which awaits you
even as you promise
to await us
beyond our death.

Fifth Week in Lent

Sunday

For though I am free with respect to all, I have made myself a slave to all, so I might win more of them. 1 Corinthians 9:19

free
to have my
way
free to bullydoze
others
out of the way

free to
choose
all the seductions
offering their
wares to me
may i willingly
prefer
to serve your
people.

Monday

*Your hands have made and
   fashioned me;
  give me understanding
   that I may learn your
   commandments.* Psalm 119:73

you take our hands,
   guiding our fingers
under your words
    sounding out the
           grace
  we have trouble pronouncing;

our friends laugh
    with opened-wide-eyes
  when they see
      the way we cling
    to your hope;

your reach up
     to lift us off
  our DIY pedestals
   so we can
        serve
   beside you
   in the dust;

cradle us
   in your constant
  heart,
     just as you
   promise.

Tuesday

You will not fear the terror
    of the night,
  or the arrow that flies by
    day,
or the pestilence that stalks
    in darkness,
  or the destruction that
    wastes at noonday. Psalm 91:5-6

the doctor's visit
  i dread,
  that sweaty-palmed
    first date;
the qualms
  that turn lunch
     into acid,
  the redundancy
  that obliterates
    my dreams;
the pandemic
    of fear
  that tap dances
  down the hall
    toward my room
    at night;
take your best shot
    everybody -
God has
  my back
    my front
  my side
    my life.

Wednesday

"All who came before me are thieves and bandits; but the sheep did not listen to them." John 10:8

we would let
the hinges rust
so the noise
would alert us
when the outsiders
try to sneak in,

but you oil the
gate
so they can
simply be welcomed;
we slam the
gate shut, as tight
(and loudly) as possible
to make our point,
yet keep finding
it open every time
you go in and out;
the despots
would keep us
confined (for our own
protection, of course)
behind their walls
made of dry fears,
but you take out your
picks, jiggling the tumblers
until they fall into place,
so we can slip through the
gate
following you into
the pastures of grace.

Thursday

So the Jews gathered around him and said to him, "How long will you keep us in suspense? If you are the Messiah, tell us plainly."
John 10:24

when it seems
   life is like
   a murder mystery
  with so many twists
  and too many characters
     to keep track
     of, you come
   underlining **grace**
   every time it appears
   in our story;
when we close
our eyes tight,
   not wanting to
   witness the horrific

      scenes on the screen
  at the World's
  reality cinema, you come
    and sit next to us,
    taking our hand,
        whispering,
  "don't be scared;
  i know how this
      ends;"
when we stumble
    in the shadows,
  groping along
  the rough walls
    of anxiety's alley,
      our finger tips
      raw and bloody
    from trying to
    find our way
    unaided, you come
  using the Spirit's peace
  to illumine our way
        home.

Friday

Mary took a pound of costly perfume made of pure nard, anointed Jesus' feet, and wiped them with her hair. The house was filled with the fragrance of the perfume. John 12:3

you waste
    yourself
  on us, showing
  us you know
we are worth
    what you
    are going
  through;
you bathe
    us
  with the costly
    perfume
of your tears,
    filling
  our hearts
  with the
    rich aroma

   of your
   love;
you pour
     your precious
   grace
      upon us,
     anointing us
     for our
       resurrection
       morning.

Saturday

The days are surely coming, says the LORD, when I will make a new covenant with the house of Israel and the house of Judah.
Jeremiah 31:31

when my eyes
     want to dart
     from one distraction
   to the next,
  may they focus
  only on you;
when my feet
     want to turn
     and flee back
   to my old
       life,
  may they follow you;
when my mind
     wants to twist
     nervously, getting
   sweatier with
   every turn,
  may it be
     emptied of
     everything but you;
as you draw
nearer to Jerusalem,
    may i have
    the foolish
       frailty
  to draw closer to
     you
in the coming days.

Holy Week

Passion/Palm Sunday

The blind and the lame came to him in the temple, and he cured them. Matthew 21:14

some are
   but children,
  hopping from one
     foot to the next,
   the flow of the
      parade
   carrying them in
   its excitement
    like a stick
    down a river;
some are
   the ignored and
   the outcast,
  hoping from one
      moment to the next,
    that maybe this time,
   this one, will carry
   them in his compassion;
some are
   palm wavers,
  hinting from one
    shout to the next,
   their longings for freedom
   carried deep within
     their souls;
some are
   passionate doubters,
  hauling their fears
  from one
    pocket to the next,
   making room
   for the nails
    handed out by
    the leaders;
all are
   simply

     us.

Monday

More than that, I regard everything as loss because of the surpassing value of knowing Christ Jesus my Lord. For his sake I have suffered the loss of all things, and I regard them as rubbish, in order that I may gain Christ   Philippians 3:8

all the
   junk
  in my life,
     i would jettison,
all the
   temptations,
  i would toss aside,
all the
   panic,
  i would pitch,
all the
   doubts,
  i would discard,
all the
   foolishness,
  i would fling away,
so i m ght
    be filled
  as you empty
    yourself
   for me.

Tuesday

"Very truly, I tell you, unless a grain of wheat falls into the earth and dies, it remains just a single grain; but if it dies, it bears much fruit."
John 12:24

that little seed
    we call
  faith
    seems to take
    so long to germinate
   and begin its journey
   of growth towards you;
those moments
    of reflection and
    solitude which

             might fill us
               with the words
                   and vitality
           to reach out to others
          seem all too
                fleeting;
     but now, your hour
           has come, and
       so may we
               serve you,
                    and in
           the serving,
               may we
           follow you
     rather than running
          away, which
       we are prone
       to do when our
            hour comes.

Wednesday

Jesus said to them, "The light is with you for a little longer. Walk while you have the light, so that the darkness may not overtake you. If you walk in the darkness, you do not know where you are going."
John 12:35

now
if only for a
      moment,
if only for
           this
      moment,
may we walk
       with you,
   Light of
       the world,
so
we may begin
    to find our
            way
   out of the
      valley of
      shadows
    we have carved
  for ourselves.

Maundy Thursday

Then he poured water into a basin and began to wash the disciples' feet and to wipe them with the towel that was tied around him.
John 13:5

seeing our
   souls
  callused by
     running
     from you,
 our hearts
   caked with
   the debris of
    our doubts,
you dip your
     hands
 into the hollow
 of your grace,
   scooping up
   your tears which
      had gathered
    there
     drop by drop,
   then
kneeling
you bathe us
  in your
    death.

Good Friday

When Jesus had received the wine, he said, "It is finished." Then he bowed his head and gave up his spirit. John 19:30

in the emptying
     of your heart,
 we taste
   your bitter
      grief;
in the silencing
     of your voice,
 we hear
   your cry of
      desertion;

in the shattering
    of your soul,
  we feel
    our brokenness
    being made
        whole.

Holy Saturday

and laid it in his own new tomb, which he had hewn in the rock. He then rolled a great stone to the door of the tomb and went away.
Matthew 27:60

as the biting
   wind of
 chaos
     moves over
     our void
Spirit
   plays a
 requiem
     on her
   baritone sax
while
  God sits
    at the piano,
  composing a
       tune
   we never
   expected.

Easter Week

Sunday

Then their eyes were opened, and they recognized him; and he vanished from their sight. Luke 24:31

on this morning

wipe away our
     tears, so
  we may see
       you
    in every stranger
    we meet;

dislodge the sounds
      of grief, so
  we may hear
      you
   in the whoops
    of excited
    children;
anoint our scarred
     souls, so
  we may welcome
     you
   into our unfurnished
     hearts.

Monday

The dead do not praise the
    LORD,
 nor do any that go down
    into silence. Psalm 115:17

you whispered into
   death's silent embrace,
  calling forth your
    child, so
we could learn new
     songs
  to praise you.

Tuesday

And when you turn to the right or when you turn to the left, your ears shall hear a word behind you, saying, "This is the way; walk in it." Isaiah 30:21

on those days when
   we seem to be stuck
   on roundabouts with
  no exits, you
    have our back,
  gently pointing us
  down the right
     way, with a

Word.

Wednesday

*As in the days when you
came out of the land of
Egypt,
show us marvelous
things.* Micah 7:15

in the encouragement
of a teacher
  for one struggling
  with math;

in the mother
who shows her son
  how to change
  a flat tire;

in the politician
who lives integrity
  over expediency,
we glimpse just a few
of your marvels.

Thursday

"No one has greater love than this, to lay down one's life for one's friends." John 15:13

perhaps
    the way we lay
    down our lives
  is to
jettison our prejudices,
stop our ears
  to damaging words,
spend more on the needy
  than on ourselves,
welcome everyone
as a friend, not
  a fear.

Friday

"But now I am going to him who sent me; yet none of you asks me, 'Where are you going?'" John 16:5

if we pay
    attention
to where you have
    been,
we might realize
that where you
    are going is
  precisely our journey's
        end.

Saturday

For you have been a refuge
        to the poor,
    a refuge to the needy in
        their distress,
    a shelter from the
        rainstorm and a shade
        from the heat. Isaiah 25:4

let the umbrella
    of our compassion
  be wide enough
  to shelter those soaked
        by poverty;
let our hearts offer
    a cool respite
    to those sweltering
  in the brutal sun
        of intolerance.

2nd Week of Easter

Sunday

Once you were not a people,
    but now you are God's
        people;
once you had not received
        mercy,
    but now you have received
        mercy. 1 Peter 2:10

you wander through
  the streets in the

    hours no one else
        does,
gathering up the orphans
sleeping rough,
    bringing them
  where they are
    fed with grace,
      wrapped in mercy,
    cradled in hope, and
know they are
      finally
  home.

Monday

We have escaped like a bird
  from the snare of the
    fowlers;
the snare is broken,
  and we have escaped. Psalm 124:7

you pick the lock
    on the cage
  where we are trapped
by our old friend death,
    and gently reaching
              in,

you pull us out
and whisper to us,
    'fly, fly!'
  releasing us into the
Spirit's breeze.

Tuesday

In the second year of Nebuchadnezzar's reign, Nebuchadnezzar dreamed such dreams that his spirit was troubled and his sleep left him. Daniel 2:1

in the wee hours
    of our fears,
as we toss and turn
our sheets wet with worry,
  you creep into our
      room,

taking us into your
>arms,
and rocking us
gently in your
>peace.

Wednesday

"I made your name known to them, and I will make it known, so that the love with which you have loved me may be in them, and I in them." John 17:26

give us grace to love
>those marginalized
>>by the powerful;
>those wounded
>>by words of hate;
>those who cannot
>>put one weary
>>foot before another;
>those who run
>>in fear, just
as you did.

Thursday

Let what you heard from the beginning abide in you. 1 John 2:24a

remind us
>that **abide**
>does not mean
letting our grace
>gather dust,
shoving compassion
>to the back
>of the closet;
thinking justice
>is a privilege
>for a select few.

Friday

Beloved, we are God's children now; what we will be has not yet been revealed. What we do know is this: when he is revealed, we will be like him, for we will see him as he is. 1 John 3:2

in those who don't have
two coins to rub together,
  but will buy a meal
  for the hungry;
in the broken-hearted
  who embrace those
  thrown aside by the world;
in the tech-savvy kid
  who reads a book
  to her neighbor every day,
we get glimpses of you
out of the corners of our eyes.

Saturday

How does God's love abide in anyone who has the world's goods and sees a brother or sister in need and yet refuses help?
1 John 3:17

words don't put
  groceries on the table;
bromides don't build
  bridges of hope;
platitudes cannot bring
  healing to the broken,
    but
    love
that breaks open piggybacks
  for an injured friend;
that raises vegetables
  for a food bank;
that confronts CEOs
  about unequal pay?
oh my!

3rd **Week of Easter**

Sunday

Above all, maintain constant love for one another, for love covers a multitude of sins. 1 Peter 4:8

we want to ration
    our love based
    on the values of
      others,

   or divide it into
    unequal piles
     which unbalance
     the scales,
or keep it locked
up in our hearts,
   as we conveniently
   lose the combination,
but you whisper,

'let it flow, let it flow,
it will never run out!'

Monday

Beloved, if our hearts do not condemn us, we have boldness before God; ⸺ John 3:21

our frigid hearts
   that refuse to weep
   for hungry children;
our bitter hearts
   that overflow
   with grudges;
our wounded hearts
   pitted by hurtful
   words we utter
      condemn us, so
gather them up
and boldly reshape them
   like yours.

Tuesday

The commandment we have from him is this: those who love God must love their brothers and sisters also. 1 John 4:21

not maybe
   or as a suggestion;

not think about it
   or write a paper;

not sometimes
   or once in a blue moon,

but ***must love***
    unconditionally
  totally
    wonderingly
just as God does.

Wednesday

Immediately the fingers of a human hand appeared and began writing on the plaster of the wall of the royal palace, next to the lampstand. The king was watching the hand as it wrote. Daniel 5:5

  no amount of
    wallpaper,
  no multi coats of
    paint,
  no pictures hung
    edge to edge
will cover your words
  justice
    hope
  peace
    grace
written on the walls
of our hearts.

Thursday

Simon answered, "Master, we have worked all night long but have caught nothing. Yet if you say so, I will let down the nets." Luke 5:5

too tired to
    keep your eyes
  open;
so weary your bones
    creak and ache;
looking with deep
    longing at your
  bed,
you
    let down your heart,
  refusing to rest
until you gather all
  into your grace.

Friday

And this is love, that we walk according to his commandments; this is the commandment just as you have heard from the beginning—you must walk in it. 2 John 6

no soft shoe
   shuffle,
  but dancing with joy
    when the prisoner
    is set free;
no tentative toes
   checking the temperature,
  but racing into
    waves when little ones'
    lives are overturned;
no turning around
   and tip-toeing
   in the other direction,
  but walking straight up
  to injustice and getting
  in its face until it backs down –
that's love!

Saturday

Beloved, you do faithfully whatever you do for the friends, even though they are strangers to you; 3 John 5

the tatted and
   pierced kid
   on the bus,
the rough sleeper
   needing a meal,
the army veteran
   desperate for a
  job,
the grandmother
   rocking on
   dementia's porch,
may be the
    very friends
  we have been
  seeking.

4th Week of Easter

Sunday

Then he said, "Oh do not let the Lord be angry if I speak just once more. Suppose ten are found there." He answered, "For the sake of ten I will not destroy it." Genesis 18:32

because you refuse
   to reduce your
     grace
  to some formula, you
always would rather
  hold dear the just
than wipe out
   the unjust.

Monday

May you be blessed by the
    LORD,
 who made heaven and
    earth. Psalm 115:15

the rain that brings
  sunburned grass
  back to life;
the little birds
  playing hide-and-seek
  with the cat;
the snow crunching
  beneath our boots
  on a winter morning –
your blessings are
always unnoticed,
    sad to say.

Tuesday

For I am with you, says the
    LORD, to save you; Jeremiah 30:11a

an introvert at
  a raucous party;
a battered woman
  in a shelter;

a child swinging
   at an empty
      playground;
an extrovert on
   a silent retreat;

we are never
  alone.

Wednesday

"But I say to you that listen, Love your enemies, do good to those who hate you," Luke 6:27

we could share
  grace with those
  who hurt us;
we could offer
  peace to our
    enemies;
we could whisper
  hope in the ears
  of crude speakers;
we could swaddle
  all damaged by hate
    with healing love,

if we but pay attention
to you.

Thursday

See to it that no one takes you captive through philosophy and empty deceit, according to human tradition, according to the elemental spirits of the universe, and not according to Christ. Colossians 2:8

break the shackles
   wrapped around our hearts
   by the purveyors of prejudice;
set us free from
  the fears offered,
  so freely, so often;
fill us with words
   of hope and grace

when we would gorge
ourselves on
the empty calories
   of broken promises.

Friday

there is hope for your future,
        says the LORD: Jeremiah 31:17a

may our **yeses**
   to your hope
 drown out the naysayers;
let us grasp
   with joy
 the days to come, rather
   than dragging the
   past behind us;
help us to follow where
   you would take us,
  instead of always
  losing our way
   with yellowed and
   outdated maps.

Saturday

As God's chosen ones, holy and beloved, clothe yourselves with compassion, kindness, humility, meekness, and patience.
Colossians 3:12

we are not handed
  tuxedos to wear down
    red carpets,
  but overalls to clean
    littered streets;
we are not fitted
  with sleek, high-priced
    sneakers,
  but sensible, silent shoes
    for walking hospital corridors;
we are not measured
  for appearances on
   talk shows, but
  garbed in smelly castoffs
  to sit with the rough sleepers.

5th *Week of Easter*

Sunday

"In everything do to others as you would have them do to you; for this is the law and the prophets." Matthew 7:12

we seek forgiveness,
   yet offer only judgment;
we long for hope,
   but deliver despair;
we hunger for grace,
   but feed our friends on fear;
we want goodness,
   but nurture mean spirits
   in our hearts.

Monday

She stood behind him at his feet, weeping, and began to bathe his feet with her tears and to dry them with her hair. Then she continued kissing his feet and anointing them with the ointment. Luke 7:38

i can cry
at the drop
of a hanky
     at
  every schmaltzy
  movie, but
have i ever
bathed you with
  my tears of
    joy,
      gratitude,
  simple love?

Tuesday

For by the grace given to me I say to everyone among you not to think of yourself more highly than you ought to think, but to think with sober judgment, each according to the measure of faith that God has assigned. Romans 12:3

why is it we are
so eager to be

   lifelong learners of
lust,
bitterness,
anger,

but think we graduated
from your academy
  of grace,
    love,
    peace,
decades ago?

Wednesday

He said to them, "Where is your faith?" Luke 8:25a

our faith?

we left it back
on the shore, worried
  it might get seasick;
it's safely locked up
in the bank vault,
  slowly drawing
  interest (we hope);
it's shoved to the
back of our hearts,
  since we are convinced
  we don't really need
to rely on it.

Thursday

We do not live to ourselves, and we do not die to ourselves.
Romans 14:7

if we live only
    to
  ourselves, we
will never taste
grace from the lemonade
stand of the kids on the corner;
    or
listen to the stories
of the people who marched
at Selma, Stonewall, or Faslane;

or
be embraced by the
love of strangers
who could care less
that we are not them.

Friday

For the kingdom of God is not food and drink but righteousness and peace and joy in the Holy Spirit. Romans 14:17

the kingdom is tasted,
not in a 5-star bistro,
  but at a shelter
  feeding families;
the kingdom is felt,
not in a cashmere
coat with a silk scarf,
  but in putting a diaper
  on a little baby;
the kingdom is found,
not in the corridors of
      power,
but in rocking chairs
on the front porch
of the retirement center.

Saturday

so that together you may with one voice glorify the God and Father of our Lord Jesus Christ. Romans 15:6

help us to stop
  arguing about
 every jot and tittle
   that tried to divide
     us,

but begin to
learn the simple
harmonies of your
 love songs of grace.

6*th* *Week of Easter*

Sunday

There will, however, be no one in need among you, because the LORD is sure to bless you in the land that the LORD God is giving you as a possession to occupy, Deuteronomy 15:4

the hungry,
  the broken,
the hurting,
  the lonely,
the unloved,
  the outcasts –

looks like you are
expecting us to take the lead
in caring for them!

Monday

No one, when tempted, should say, "I am being tempted by God"; for God cannot be tempted by evil and he himself tempts no one. James 1:13

but it is so
    much easier
    to blame you,
dear God,
    for the trouble
    we cause
    ourselves, rather
  than looking in the
      mirror!

Tuesday

You must understand this, my beloved: let everyone be quick to listen, slow to speak, slow to anger; James 1:19

if we would spend
  more time listening
    to others,
      to our hearts,
    to you,
we might not be
so quick to let

words tumble out of
    our mouths,
and anger rush
pell-mell from our
    hearts.

Wednesday

He said to his disciples, "Therefore I tell you, do not worry about your life, what you will eat, or about your body, what you will wear."
Luke 12:22

we spend so much time
    worrying about tomorrow,
    we often miss today;
we are so obsessed
    with six-pack abs
    and fitting into skinny jeans,
  we forget to play
  in the sprinklers with
    the kids;
we are so busy pouring over the ingredients
of every item in the basket,
  we don't taste the juicy tomato,
  bite into a sweet apple,
  savor a cold glass of milk.

Eve of Ascension

Elijah said to him, "Elisha, stay here; for the LORD has sent me to Jericho." But he said, "As the LORD lives, and as you yourself live, I will not leave you." So they came to Jericho. 2 Kings 2:4

we lie awake
    listening to the murmurs
  of those who tell
    us
      over and over
      that we are on
      our own, and
so miss your gentle
  assurance that you
  will always be with

        us.

Ascension Day

*God has gone up with a
    shout,
  the LORD with the sound of
    a trumpet;* Psalm 47:5

you go up with
  a shout, but
  we still hear you
  in the laughter of
    children;

trumpets herald
  your way,
while an oboe solo
  reminds us of your
  presence in our grief;

we stand looking into
  the sky, waiting,
  while you have set
off down the road
to be with the
  dispossessed.

Friday

*Why should I fear in times of
  trouble;* Psalm 49:5a

the naysayers may
  mock me,
the radio callers
  may rip me
  to pieces,
the late night hosts
  may make me
  the punch line of all their
    comedy routines, but
i am going
to let go of my
    fear
and grab hold of
your hand.

Saturday

"Let these words sink into your ears: The Son of Man is going to be betrayed into human hands." Luke 9:44

when we will not
    lift a finger
    to help another;
when we refuse to
  cross the street
  to mend a broken
      friendship;
when we close our
    minds to hope
  and wonder,
we continue
to betray
    you.

7th Week of Easter

Sunday

"Whoever welcomes you welcomes me, and whoever welcomes me welcomes the one who sent me." Matthew 10:40

when we are convinced
    we should build walls,
  remove the welcome
  mat from the door step,
    set restrictions on
    refugee families,
remind us
    who
  we might be
  turning away.

Monday

When the days drew near for him to be taken up, he set his face to go to Jerusalem. Luke 9:51

while we close
our eyes to the
lonely fellow on the bus,

    you go and sit
    next to him;
when we turn
our backs on the
hungry and broken,
    you open wide
    your arms to them;
though we can't face
the injustices around us,
    you go nose-to-nose
    with them until they
melt away from your
        hope.

Tuesday

He said to them, "The harvest is plentiful, but the laborers are few; therefore ask the Lord of the harvest to send out laborers into his harvest." Luke 10:2

there always seems
to be a bumper
        crop
 of injustices, so
shake us out of
our apathy, reminding
us that, together,
we can bring hope
to all choked by
    the weeds of
    oppression.

Wednesday

I will give them one heart, and put a new spirit within them; I will remove the heart of stone from their flesh and give them a heart of flesh, Ezekiel 11:19

our fears reduce
our hearts to
    ice crystals;
our prejudices always
seem to be recycled
    into bitter hearts;
we have no problem
reusing the angry words

    which are shaped
    in the dankness
    of our hearts;
so make us one
  with that heart
  of grace and love
which s you.

Thursday

Know that all lives are mine; Ezekiel 18:4a

when we would warehouse
the mentally ill in prisons
      or
move foster kids
from house to house,
  their lives and memories
  carried in garbage bags
    or
build grand mansions
where an aging population
can live in style (though
      forgotten),
remind us
  (and it will take
  more than once),
    that these are
your children, entrusted
to our care.

Friday

Is it not enough for you to feed on the good pasture, but you must tread down with your feet the rest of your pasture? When you drink of clear water, must you foul the rest with your feet? Ezekiel 34:18

we use power
  to move people
  aside in order to
  build bigger bigs;
we convince
  ourselves our
  emissions will not
  bother asthmatics;

we divert the
  best water to
  expensive resorts,
    while children
    drink lead:
have mercy on us,
good Lord,
have mercy on us.

Saturday

In old age they still produce
    fruit;
  they are always green and
    full of sap, Psalm 92:14

parkinsoned hands
  can still help
  build homes for others;
dimmed eyes
  can tell story after
  story to little kids;
weakened voices
  are able to
  cry out for justice;
fading ears
  listen to the
  whispers of hope,
if we would just
stop writing the formula:
aging = uselessness

Eve of Pentecost

Tremble, O earth, at the
    presence of the LORD,
  at the presence of the God
    of Jacob, Psalm 114:7

while we curl
up warm and cozy
in our beds, Ruach
    lies awake, trembling
with anticipation of
blowing all our
  worries,

    prejudices,
  foolishness out
the windows of our souls.

Pentecost

The voice of the LORD causes
    the oaks to whirl,
  and strips the forest bare;
  and in his temple all say,
    "Glory!" Psalm 29:9

you sing,
  and we join hands
    with strangers,
  twirling around on the
    dance floor;

you whisper, and
  we hear the
  cries of hungry
    children;

you shout, and
  strip away all
  our fears, so we
can cry
    Justice!
    Peace!
    Hope!
to all around us.

For the following weekdays, readings are taken from the week which corresponds to the date of Pentecost.

Eve of Trinity Sunday

Lord, you have been our
    dwelling place
  in all generations. Psalm 90:1

while we burn
the midnight oil, trying
  to come up with
  the correct formula
  to explain youyouyou,

Spirit is in the
   kitchen, preparing
   a full breakfast;
Jesus is running
   the bed linens through
   the washer and dryer;
and Abba is sweeping
   off the front porch,
just as youyouyou
   have always done.

Trinity Sunday

Keep these words that I am commanding you today in your heart.
Deuteronomy 6:6

may we whisper of
your love, O God,
   to our children,
   until it becomes
   their most trusted
      adviser;

may we slip our
hands under your compassion,
      Servant of the Poor,
   so we may carry
   hope to the lonely,
      healing to the broken;

may we keep you
in our hearts, Kind Spirit,
   so in every moment,
   day or night, we
offer your grace.

On the following weekdays, reading are taken from the week which corresponds to the date of Trinity Sunday.

Week following Sunday between May 11 and 16 inclusive, if after Pentecost Sunday

Monday

*It was no messenger or
      angel*

> *but his presence that saved
> them;
> in his love and in his pity he
> redeemed them;
> he lifted them up and
> carried them all the
> days of old.* Isaiah 63:9

it wasn't a pen-and-ink
   costumed crusader
      or
   strident, boastful
      politician;
it wasn't a weapons
toting equalizer
      or
   spinning dervish
   with flying hands and feet,
    but
grace born into poverty,
compassion bent by suffering,
a Word covered with flung curses,
love torn apart by hate
     who
   saved us.

Tuesday

May the Lord grant mercy to the household of Onesiphorus, because he often refreshed me and was not ashamed of my chain; when he arrived in Rome, he eagerly searched for me and found me
2 Timothy 1:16-17

we drag our feet
  heading toward the
  shelter needing volunteers;
we wait to see if
the sign-up sheet
for prison visits gets filled
  before we go near it;

we are reluctant
to march against weapons
that can destroy the world,
    and so,

never feel the breeze
as you rush by
to offer mercy to
any one and every one.

Wednesday

Remind them of this, and warn them before God that they are to avoid wrangling over words, which does no good but only ruins those who are listening. 2 Timothy 2:14

we can throw a rope
around words of compassion
and hogtie them until they
holler,
     "Uncle!"
we can pile arguments
on tables until they
sag under the weight
  of animosity,   or
we could listen to
your heart and rest
in comfortable silence.

Thursday

"Then he said, 'I will do this: I will pull down my barns and build larger ones, and there I will store all my grain and my goods.'" Luke 12:18

if
we spent as much time
  building shelters for the homeless,
  schools for kids who need them,
  clinics for those without insurance
instead
  of more barns so we
  can have more stuff,
     people
might just pay attention
to who we say we follow.

Friday

"Do not be afraid, little flock, for it is your Father's good pleasure to give you the kingdom." Luke 12:32

   when fear no
     longer has a tight
     grasp on your
       heart,
can you begin
to imagine
    the wonders you
    would discover
within?

Saturday

So I have looked upon you in
    the sanctuary,
  beholding your power and
    glory. Psalm 63:2

i look for you
down power's corridors,
  but you are changing
  the linens at the hospice;
i look for you at
the gala of celebrities,
              but
  you are teaching
  refugees a new language;
I look for you in
high-tech church campuses,
  but you are sleeping
  rough with your
     children
on the sidewalks.

Week following Sunday between May 17 and 23 inclusive, if after Pentecost Sunday

Monday

In the days when the judges ruled, there was a famine in the land,
Ruth 1:1a

if there is a famine
  of faith, could
  it be we have
  stopped trusting;

if there is a misery
  of mercy, have
  we stored it in
  our hearts until
  it dried up;
if there is a hardship
  of hope, could it be
  we lost the seeds
entrusted to us?

Tuesday

And just then there appeared a woman with a spirit that had crippled her for eighteen years. She was bent over and was quite unable to stand up straight. Luke 13:11

too often, we
  walk by folks
bent from grudges,
    dreads,
    rejections,
thinking only an expert
can help them, while
all they need is   a friend.

Wednesday

And again he said, "To what should I compare the kingdom of God? It is like yeast that a woman took and mixed in with three measures of flour until all of it was leavened." Luke 13:20-21

the kingdom is
like hope that is
  mixed in with
  equal measures of justice,
so people may rise
up out of poverty
to claim the lives
taken away by others.

Thursday

*I say to the LORD, "You are
    my Lord;
  I have no good apart from
    you."* Psalm 16:2

i looked for the good
　in empty promises,
　but they slipped
　through my soul;
i thought i found
　goodness in wealth,
　but only ended up
　in debt to worry;
i searched for first-class
　treatment from others,
　but got bullied
　for my choices.

then you reached
　　　　out
　to gather me close,
your grace gluing
us together forever.

Friday

The women of the neighborhood gave him a name, saying, "A son has been born to Naomi." They named him Obed; he became the father of Jesse, the father of David. Ruth 4:17

sometimes
it is the
　　skeletons
　in our closet
　　(like Ruth) who
gave life,
　hope,
　　grace,
to those they
would never meet.

Saturday

"But when you give a banquet, invite the poor, the crippled, the lame, and the blind." Luke 14:13

let us
forget the powerful
　and make friends
　with the poor;

stop trying to catch up
to the celebs
   and learn dance steps
   from the disabled;
give up on rubbing elbows
with the executives,
   to share a picnic
   with those who
   empty our bins.

Week following Sunday between May 24 and 28 inclusive, if after Pentecost Sunday

Sunday

But take care and watch yourselves closely, so as neither to forget the things that your eyes have seen nor to let them slip from your mind all the days of your life; make them known to your children and your children's children-- Deuteronomy 4:9

careless,
   we ignore the signs
   of caution, and drive
   over the abyss into apathy;
slipshod,
   we stubbornly forget
   all your words of grace
   and speak harshly to
      all around us;
negligent,
   we are too busy
   with our devices to
   tell our kids about
     prodigals,
     samaritans, and
a baby born
     just like them.

Monday

who consoles us in all our affliction, so that we may be able to console those who are in any affliction with the consolation with which we ourselves are consoled by God. 2 Corinthians 1:4

because we have
been comforted,

    we can embrace
        others;
because we have
been helped,
  we are able to
  reach out a hand
        to the fallen;
because we have
been forgiven,
    we must . . .

Tuesday

Now all the tax collectors and sinners were coming near to listen to him. Luke 15:1

now,
    why
 in the world
do we arrogantly
    (stubbornly)
believe Jesus
has nothing to
      say
  to us?

Wednesday

Then he became angry and refused to go in. His father came out and began to plead with him. Luke 15:28

we will
        never
  hear
     understand
    live
this story, until
we realize
    we
  are neither the

    prodigal
      nor
    papa.

Thursday

Then we will never turn
*   back from you;*
* give us life, and we will*
*   call on your name.* Psalm 80:18

lock those clear,
   piercing
         eyes
 of grace and
     hope
onto our weary
    ones, until
we realize we have
no need to look
      back
 on our foolishness,
but can whisper your
         name
  from this moment on:

     Love

Friday

you shall have no other gods before me. Deuteronomy 5:7

so casual we don't
  notice the bend
  in the road;
so comfortable
  they fit like
  faded jeans;
so easy to please,
  it takes no effort
  on our part –
no wonder
we would rather
be held captive
by those gods
who care nothing for

        us.

Saturday

"There was a rich man who was dressed in purple and fine linen and who feasted sumptuously every day. And at his gate lay a poor man named Lazarus, covered with sores," Luke 16:19-20

all we have to do is
  share the clothes
  we no longer wear
         (or fit!);
fill up a grocery bag
  for the food pantry;
volunteer to help
  refugees relocate
  successfully, but
it is so much easier
to ignore Lazarus,
  wherever,
    whoever,
      whenever.

Week following Sunday between May 29 and June 4 inclusive, if after Pentecost Sunday

Sunday

And they took offense at him. Matthew 13:57a

we take offense at
  the poor, when they
    could bless us with hope;
  the outsiders, who
    could teach us the
    ropes about endurance;
  the single moms, who
    model the love
    we all need;
  you, because you
    are you.

Monday

If you will only heed his every commandment that I am commanding you today – loving the LORD your God, and serving him with all your heart and with all your soul -- Deuteronomy 11:13

we keep the rulebook
in our back pocket,
ready to pull it out
  and point out
  every single infraction,
but loving you
with every cell,
  serving others with
  our hearts, souls,
  hands, and feet?
we never seem
to pay attention, do we?

Tuesday

We are putting no obstacle in anyone's way, so that no fault may be found with our ministry, 2 Corinthians 6:3

we put up detour signs
to keep others from
    finding peace, but
    you paint arrows over
    them, to show the way;
we put banana peels
on the sidewalk so
  folks will slip
  on their foolishness,
but you catch them
to set them back on their feet.

Wednesday

Make room in your hearts for us; 2 Corinthians 7:2a

our hearts filled
with so many grudges,
  so many lusts,
  so many memories
    of hurts we cause,
we have no room
for those who
are looking for hope,
  or for you, who
could transform us
into guest houses for
    our sisters and brothers.

Thursday

"And will not God grant justice to his chosen ones who cry to him day and night? Will he delay long in helping them?" Luke 18:7

we keep trying to derail
your attempts to bring
justice to those
    whose pleas for hope
    we ignore,
but you just laugh
at our futile efforts
       and
invite us to join you
in rebuilding
    reconciliation.

Friday

"The Pharisee, standing by himself, was praying thus, 'God, I thank you that I am not like other people: thieves, rogues, adulterers, or even like this tax collector.'" Luke 18:11

we thank you,
that like
  ex-hackers who teach
    computer skills to
    senior citizens,
  prisoners who turn
    rescue dogs into
    therapists,
  and even frail,
  foolish folks like us

you
  are the
    God
of second chances.

Saturday

People were bringing even infants to him that he might touch them; and when the disciples saw it, they sternly ordered them not to do it. Luke 18:15

you come, your light
of grace burning bright,
so the invisible ones;
   the kids huddled in
      poverty's doorways,
   the older folks on
    fixed incomes,
   the parents working
    three jobs,
   the cleaners of
    our resort rooms,
can be seen
     clearly
as our sisters and brothers.

Week following Sunday between June 5 and 11 inclusive, if after Pentecost Sunday

Sunday

*Even though I walk through
   the darkest valley,
 I fear no evil;* Psalm 23:4a

through the murkiness
  of menial work,
the hospital in
  the dread of night,
the obscurity of
  tomorrow's worries,
the twilight of
  dwindling years –
you are with us
  every step
    every moment
  every where.

Monday

Look at what is before your eyes. 2 Corinthians 10:7a

your joy is before us
  in kids playing hopscotch;
your peace is revealed
  in 90-year-olds
  holding hands;

your imagination
  flickers in fireflies;
your grace caresses
  us in summer breezes,
if we but open our
      eyes.

Tuesday

So he ran ahead and climbed a sycamore tree to see him, because he was going to pass that way. When Jesus came to the place, he looked up and said to him, "Zacchaeus, hurry and come down; for I must stay at your house today." Luke 19:4-5

when we run   ahead
  to climb our favorite
  tree to watch temptation's
     parade come down
    the street,
  you look up,
and call out, "jump
down into my arms;
   i'll show you
   something really
   neat to see!"

Wednesday

*let the field exult, and
    everything in it.
Then shall all the trees of the
    forest sing for joy Psalm 96:12*

you pick up
   the baton, and
  with a flick of
  your wrist, flowers
begin to hum the tune,
  birds twitter the melody,
and the choir of oaks,
  elms, redwoods, and pines
   burst into a great
  cantata of creation
   for all to hear
   for all time.

Thursday

He answered, "I tell you, if these were silent, the stones would shout out." Luke 19:40

when we remain
       close-mouthed
  as the strident
  shouts of the
    immigrant-slanderers
    fear-mongers
    vulnerable-deriders
  race through our
       communities,
may we hear
the stones cry out,
  'use us to build
    bridges of compassion,
    roads paved with trust,
    hospitals for the broken,
    schools filled with tolerance.'

Friday

You have ravished my heart,
    my sister, my bride,
  you have ravished my
    heart with a glance of
    your eyes,
  with one jewel of your
    necklace. Song of Solomon 4:9

spellbind my heart
    with your words
    of wonder, so i
  may dance through
  this day;

transport my heart
    to where yours
    weeps for the
  hungry, the lonely,
  the despairing,
so i
    may embrace them
    in your hope;

magnetize my heart
    drawing all the
    broken pieces
  together, the scar
 tissue the peace which
makes me whole;

entrance my heart
    once again
  with your grace,
that it will be
    yours
forever.

Saturday

Set me as a seal upon your
    heart,
 as a seal upon your arm;
for love is strong as death,
 passion fierce as the grave.
Its flashes are flashes of fire,
  a raging flame.   Song of Solomon 8:6

tattoo your grace
    upon my heart,
 so i may carry
      it
  to everyone i meet,
 especially
    those i think
    you do not care about;
wrap your faithbit
    around my soul,
 until i gradually
  grow strong enough
  to follow you
     down every rocky hurt,
      over every insurmountable
        struggle, to find
 you waiting for me
 at the end,
your passionate love
  turning death into
     dust.

Week following Sunday between June 12 and 18 inclusive

Sunday

"Whoever becomes humble like this child is the greatest in the kingdom of heaven." Matthew 18:4

let me slip
    off my
  handcrafted-from-the-finest-pride
    shoes
          and
run barefoot
  through the sprinklers
  of living water
  into the joy

    of your kingdom.

Monday

"Do not regard your servant as a worthless woman, for I have been speaking out of my great anxiety and vexation all this time."
I Samuel 1:16

the dad
    with the car full
    of kids, broken
  down by the side
  of the road;
the transgendered teen
    with a life full
    of bullies at
  school and home;
the mom
    with a fist full
    of prescriptions
  and an empty purse:

remind me
    that i am but
  an intercessor for
  their anxieties
    and a
    conduit
  for your grace.

Tuesday

As a deer longs for flowing streams,
  so my soul longs for you, O God. Psalm 42:1

as a kitten
    scours
  the house for a
  sunbeam
    on a stormy day;

as a dog
    bounces
  for just one more
  throw of the
        ball;

as a child
    wishes
  for one last
  bedtime story;

as a grandparent
    craves
  one extra day
  of Nana camp;

so i hanker
    for you,
  O God.

Wednesday

'In the last days it will be,
      God declares,
    that I will pour out my Spirit
      upon all flesh,
     and your sons and your
        daughters shall
        prophesy,
     and your young men shall
        see visions,
     and your old men shall
        dream dreams.' Acts 2:16

the teenager
> stays up past
> the setting of
> the moon, notating
> the final chords
>> for the song
>> supporting
> amnesty seekers;
the old couple
> wakes up before
> dawn, dragging
>> all those luxuries
>> they never dreamed
>> would be theirs
> out onto the lawn
> for the yard sale
> to benefit pediatric cancer;
the little boy
patiently sits at the
> computer,
> certain he can
> create an app
>> providing a
>> safe place for
>> his bullied friends
>> to voice their
> fears;
and the
> Spirit
> rejoices.

Thursday

*For you do not give me up to
Sheol,
or let your faithful one see
the Pit.* Psalm 16:10

after another of
an endless parade
> of nights
> sampling Chef Beelzebul's
> latest plates of rich food,
> and drinking sin's
> fancy cocktails
>> made especially

        for me,
i pour myself
into your taxi,
  handing you my
  address, settling
    back for a nap,
not noticing the
side streets you
     are taking,
  until you stop
  in front of
    Grace's Nite Owl
    Diner
  where you walk
  me to the front door
    whispering, 'this
is where you need
to hang out.'

Friday

they would sell their possessions and goods and distribute the proceeds to all, as any had need. Acts 2:45

we do not give
   because we have
   more luxuries
  than we need,
     but because there
     are those who
   do not enjoy
   the necessities
     of life;
  a brother is hungry,
  a sister needs chemo,
  a cousin is unjustly imprisoned,
  a child needs clothes
    and books for school,
and so,
we do not partner
with the needy
    to put a dent
     in a problem,

  but because they are family.

Saturday

He has remembered his
*   steadfast love and*
*   faithfulness*
to the house of Israel. Psalm 98:3a

you could keep
  a scrapbook with
  postcards from all
 the places we have gone
 in running from you;
you could cling
   tightly to that grudge
   that winds around
 your feet, purring
 'pick me up;'
you could lie awake
at night re-hearing
   those hurtful words
   we fling at your
 heart;
but no . . .

you remember
that covenant
  written on
  your heart;
you look at
our faces
  engraved on
  your palms;

you whisper
the vows made
  on a mountaintop
   in the wilderness,
  on a starry night
   over Bethlehem,
  on a garbage dump
   outside Jerusalem.

you remember . . .

Week following Sunday between June 19 and 25 inclusive

Sunday

But who can detect their
    errors?
  Clear me from hidden
    faults. Psalm 19:12

the classmate who
    finished diagramming
  the sentence on the board;
the math tutor who
    patiently showed
    me (over and over)
  the correct formula
  to solve the problem;
the professor whose
    red pen shaped
    me into a better
  thinker . . .
all great teachers;

but those thoughts
    which could
    wipe out a nation;
  those lusts
    which could
    destroy another's
      family;
  those fears
    which can
    turn me into
      someone different?

only you
  can help me
  graduate into
 grace.

Monday

"So also, when you see these things taking place, you know that the kingdom of God is near." Luke 21:31

when the West Bank
  wall is torn down

   and rebuilt into
   schools and hospitals;
when the Confederate
     flag is taken off
     the pole;
when bullies
     transform into
     mentors for
   little children;
when politicians
     set down their ideologies
   and stand side by side
   welcoming asylum seekers;
when the needy
     are offered leadership
     positions in the
     anti-poverty programs,
then
   we will know.

Tuesday

So he consented and began to look for an opportunity to betray him to them when no crowd was present. Luke 22:6

in the choir,
    i join in harmonizing
   about love, peace, and
       hope, but
  on the way home,
  my heart resounds with
     the songs of despair,
     anger, and cruelty;
at the church dinners,
   i curb my appetites (only
     visiting the dessert
     table once), but
  on the way home,
  i will stop at the
     fast-sin outlet
    and gorge to my
    heart's delight;
in the crowd,
   i join in affirming
   who you are, but
  walking home alone,

   i know who i
      truly am and
   what i do all too often.

Wednesday

Then Samuel took a stone and set it up between Mizpah and Jeshanah, and named it Ebenezer; for he said, "Thus far the LORD has helped us." 1 Samuel 7:12

the street sign
    bearing the name
    of the principal
   who always had
   more time for
      kids
    than for the
    paperwork;
the fresh flowers
placed in the
     vase everyday
  in front of the
  gravestone of the
    partner who fought
    to marry the man
      he loved;
the bone-shaped
   urn filled with the
   memories and heart
    of the dog
   who got her
   family
    out of the burning
    house before she
  could;

your helpers
surround us, O God.

Thursday

"But I am among you as one who serves." Luke 22:27c

in the weary
   woman

       who picks up our
            wet towels
        and empties
        the waste cans
    of our detritus
            when we vacate
            the room . . .
in the teenager
            who cleans
            the restaurant
    tables,
            throwing out
            enough food
        to feed his younger
        siblings . . .
in the octogenarian
            grandmother
    who spends her
    summer mornings
        helping six-year-olds
        hone their reading
            gifts . . .
we find you.

Friday

He had a son whose name was Saul, a handsome young man.
There was not a man among the people of Israel more handsome
than he; he stood head and shoulders above everyone else.
1 Samuel 9:2

when we look
    at the chiseled chin,
    the piercing blue eyes,
        the wind-swept hair
    and think,
        'that's the one!'
    remind us to look
    for the warts;
when we admire
    those who stand
    head and shoulders
    above the rest,
    point our eyes down
    so we can see
        the feet of   clay.

Saturday

Let them praise his name
 with dancing,
 making melody to him
 with tambourine and
 lyre. Psalm 149:3

for dogs-splashing-in-puddles
 days,
for winds
 that make kites
 swoop and float
 in the sky,

for hens
 teaching their
 ducklings
 to glide across
 the water without
 leaving a
 trail,

for fathers
 who take their
 daughters
 to work
 and mothers
 who prepare
 their two-left-footed
 sons for the
 school dance,

we praise you,
Joyous God!

Week following June 26 and July 2 inclusive

Sunday

God is our refuge and
 strength,
 a very present help in
 trouble. Psalm 46:1

    the eight-year-old
      who sits in the
      lounge of the
           Memory Unit
        patiently guiding
        her grandmother's
           finger under
        the words of
        the easy reader,
          sounding out the
        words her nana
    first learned 80+ years
      ago;
the vet
      whose tears
    join ours as
      we help our
      best friend
        cross
    the rainbow bridge;
the stranger
    who hands the
    grocery clerk
  enough cash to
  pay for the mother
      behind him
    who is scrabbling
    through her pockets
  hoping she has enough
      to buy the food
    her children need;
your help
  is always with us,
      God of the weak,
even when we
don't notice.

Monday

The Lord turned and looked at Peter. Then Peter remembered the word of the Lord, how he had said to him, "Before the cock crows today, you will deny me three times." Luke 22:61

sitting outside at
the corner café,
    you sip your tea,

      listening as
        an executive calls
        his wife to tell
          her he will be
          working late,
    all the while holding
   hands with his secretary;
you watch
the café manager
      dressing down
      the young server
    for not earning enough
   in gratuities, then
        opening up the
        register to pocket
        a handful of bills;
you notice the
church leaders
        carefully skirting
        the hungry homeless
        on the sidewalks,
   as they rush from
   their hotels to the
   convention center
     for their fully catered
     breakfast;
then you fold up
your newspaper,
   leave a gracious tip,
and walk home
to your apartment,

      dropping bitter tears
      along the way.

Tuesday

Do not drag me away with
      the wicked,
with those who are
      workers of evil,
who speak peace with their
      neighbors,
  while mischief is in their
      hearts. Psalm 28:3

we speak
> peace,
all while
we manufacture
> WMDs
in our hearts;
we whisper
> hope,
as we plant
> despair
in the gardens
of our friends'
souls;
we sing
> thanksgivings,
continually grumbling
in our greedy minds
of our empty
> lives.

Wednesday

But they were insistent and said, "He stirs up the people by teaching throughout all Judea, from Galilee where he began even to this place." Luke 23:5

stir us up
with your words
of compassion
until
we are willing
to be broken
to bring healing
to our communities;
shake us out
of our apathy,
so we might
stand in
solidarity
with those
ignored by
our world;
turn our prejudices
upside down
so we can
use them as
soap boxes

    to call for
        justice
for those who have
  none.

Thursday

Then they all shouted out together, "Away with this fellow! Release Barabbas for us!" Luke 23:18

away with this
    gift called Peace,
  release War for us!
away with this
    hope called Compassion,
  unleash Bitterness
      instead!
away with this
    grace called Love,
  let loose Hate
  in our midst!
away with this
    fellow called Jesus,

  deliver us into
    our own Foolishness!

Friday

He asked, "Who are you, Lord?" The reply came, "I am Jesus, whom you are persecuting." Acts 9:5

i am
    the transgender teen
  you won't let
  your kids befriend;

i am
    the slow-moving senior
  you nudge aside
  to get to the cashier
      first;
i am
    the frazzled mom

wondering if she
    has enough fuel
      to get her child
      to the doctor, that
you are tailgating
for not going 10 miles
over the speed limit;

i am
    the veteran
you want to serve
multiple tours in
a war zone, but
    won't give 10 minutes
    for a job interview.

i am . . .

Saturday

Then he said, "Jesus, remember me when you come into your kingdom." Luke 23:42

when
    i pave my own
  path with
    the bricks
    of my desires;
when
    the certitude
    of my convictions
  keeps me from
    living in your
    unknown future;
when
    i expect nothing
  but the best
  from others, yet
    offer them
    the worst of me;

remember me,
and bring me
  into the kingdom
of your self-giving
    love.

Week following Sunday between July 3 and 9 inclusive

Sunday

Therefore, since we are justified by faith, we have peace with God through our Lord Jesus Christ, Romans 5:1

at the end
    of that
  day we call   life,
we find you
    waiting on
    the front porch,
  offering us a
      cool drink,
    and a booming,
'welcome home!'

Monday

For the needy shall not
    always be forgotten,
  nor the hope of the poor
    perish forever. Psalm 9:18

when we ask the server
    to remove the
    half-full plate while
  the hungry scavenge
  the bins outside
      the kitchen door;
when we do not notice
    the family sleeping
    under the bridge
  on our way to look
  at a house with more
      bathrooms than
    are needed;
when we stockpile
    more and more
    of everything we
    already have,
  as more and more
    children slip into
      poverty,

recall us to your
    heart
  so we may
  stop dashing
  the hopes of
our sisters and brothers
we forget more often
    than we do   you.

Tuesday

'For the poor who are oppressed
  and the needy who groan,
I myself will arise,' says the LORD. Psalm 12:5 (*The Grail*)

while we moan and
  stretch, thinking of
every excuse to stay
  in comfort,
you slip on your
  dusty and faded
work clothes to spend
  another day building
your kingdom where
    everyone gets
  three squares a day
and that place they
can call
      home.

Wednesday

Then their eyes were opened, and they recognized him; Luke 24:31a

with the eyes
    of success,
  we cannot see
      the failures
    who get up
    every morning
  to try once more
  to be
      faithful;

with the eyes
    of wealth,

         we cannot see
             the poor
         who offer
             the little they have
         to those who have
                 less;

with the eyes
    of power,
    we cannot see
        the most vulnerable
    who can teach us
            true strength;

without the eyes
    of Easter,
how will we ever
see you take us
    bless us,
        break us,
and give us

    to others?

Thursday

"Look at my hands and my feet; see that it is I myself. Touch me and see; for a ghost does not have flesh and bones as you see that I have." Luke 24:39

show us your
    hands
  so we may use
    ours
        for the healing
      of the broken;
show us your
    feet
  so we may
    walk
      with those
      left in the lurch
  by everyone rushing by;
show us your
    heart

      so we may
        love
          those jilted
        by the world;
touch us with your
    peace
  so we may become
        intercessors
  for those who are
    bone of your bone,
    flesh of your flesh.

Friday

Lead me in your truth, and
      teach me,
  for you are the God of my
    salvation;
  for you I wait all day long. Psalm 25:5

i hung around
    while yesterday
  slid into
      today;
i rested
    while today
  impatiently
      raced towards
    tomorrow;
i will bide my time
  tomorrowandtomorrowandtomorrow,
until
i realize
    you had grown
    tired of
    waiting
        for me,
and showed up
    long
    before i
    was ready.

Saturday

and saying, "The time is fulfilled, and the kingdom of God has come near; repent, and believe in the good news." Mark 1:15

did i miss it?

the peace
   that could have
 been mine, but
     i was too busy
     arguing with myself;
the grace
   that could have
   scarred over my
 seeping grudges, but
     i was too busy
     pouring salt into
   them;
the place
   where i could
   be living - this
      very moment! - but
    i chose to
    purchase a loft
 on Sinful Street?

Week following Sunday between July 10 and 16 inclusive

Sunday

When David had finished speaking to Saul, the soul of Jonathan was bound to the soul of David, and Jonathan loved him as his own soul.
1 Samuel 18:1

give us
     patience
  until we find
     the
 friend,
   lover,
    partner
whose soul
is twinned to ours
and we become
  complete.

Monday

When he came and saw the grace of God, he rejoiced, Acts 11:23a

remind us
that grace
   is not the trophy
   we earn for winning
      the race, but
the baton
we pass on,
   laughing with delight
as it is carried
into the far distance.

Tuesday

It is like the precious oil on
      the head,
  running down upon the
     beard,
on the beard of Aaron,
  running down over the
     collar of his robes. Psalm 133:2

   community

is like tears
running down the faces
  of strangers, whose hearts
break on hearing
   of the deaths
   of more innocents
at the hands of
hate and fear.

Wednesday

"And no one puts new wine into old wineskins; otherwise, the wine will burst the skins, and the wine is lost, and so are the skins; but one puts new wine into fresh wineskins." Mark 2:22

those old,
cracked wineskins
   sewn out of
  our prejudices,
    doubts,
   and easy assumptions
just can't contain
your marvelous

    vintage of
        grace, hope, and
welcome for all.

Thursday

He looked around at them with anger; he was grieved at their hardness of heart and said to the man, "Stretch out your hand." He stretched it out, and his hand was restored. Mark 3:5

to the teenage girl,
you say,
    'stretch out
    your loneliness,'
  as you befriend her;

to the homeless family,
you invite,
  'stretch out
  your hunger,'
 as you feed them;

to the parents
at the graveside
of their child,
you whisper,
   'stretch out
   your grief,'
 as you gather
 their tears and
 drink them;

to the enemies,
you challenge,
   'stretch out
   your weapons,'
 as you transform them
 into musical instruments;

to us,
you hope,
   'stretch out
   your hardened hearts,'
 as you melt
     them.

Friday

*I pour out my complaint
before him;
I tell my trouble before
him.* Psalm 142:2

24/7
    you sit at the counter,
  your cup of tea
growing colder,
      as you listen
    to the litany
    of lament after
        lament,
  always ending with
  if-only-my-life-was-like-so-and-so's;
you wipe our tears
  with your red bandana
and as you send us
on our way with a hug,
      you think to yourself,
  'if you only knew
  what so-and-so
  was going through'

Saturday

And looking at those who sat around him, he said, "Here are my mother and my brothers!" Mark 3:34

the pierced and
    tattooed server
  who looks nothing
  like our mind's portrait
    of a proper
    young lady;
the addict
    whose jittery walk
  causes us to cross
  quickly to the other
    side of the street;
the widow who
    sits in the
    shadowed loneliness
  of her front porch

      while neighbors
      host a cookout
    for everyone else;
the immigrant
  greeting us at
  the megastore
 while his doctoral
 diploma gathers
    dust in
  the apartment
  closet . . .
your sisters
and brothers
in our midst
  that we so
  easily
dismiss.

Week following Sunday between July 17 and 23 inclusive

Sunday

O the depth of the riches and wisdom and knowledge of God! How unsearchable are his judgments and how inscrutable his ways!
Romans 11:33

i discover your
    judgment
  in the parent
  who forgives the
    child
    who continually
     breaks her heart;

i glimpse your
    riches
  in the rising creek
  after a summer storm,
   in the angels
   pressed in the snow
     by my dog;

i fathom your
    way
  in the daughter

    who patiently
    answers the same question
    asked over and over
      by her aged father;

i sense your
    wisdom
  in the purring
  of the cat
    in my lap;

i know
    you
  in the heartbeat
  next to me
    as i sleep
    through the night.

Monday

And he said to them, "To you has been given the secret of the kingdom of God, but for those outside, everything comes in parables;" Mark 4:11

in the sister
    who patiently
  teaches her little
  brother how to
    play jacks;
in the coach
    who stays until
    the fireflies appear,
  helping the girl
  learn how to bend
      the ball;
in the teacher
    who spends her
    summer days
  getting ready
  for her new class,
we begin to
    solve
  that mystery
    which stumps
  so many armchair
      detectives.

Tuesday

Teach me your way, O LORD,
   that I may walk in your
      truth;
   give me an undivided heart
      to revere your name. Psalm 86:11

i gladly offer
   my listening heart
   to the politician
   with the seductive
      words;
i give away
   my aching heart
   to every huckster
   with a magic pill
      or new-and-improved
      solution;
i toss
   my broken heart
   to every empty person
   who promises
      to return it
      full of love;
and so   i
   have nothing left
   to offer   you.

Wednesday

When they arrived, they called the church together and related all that God had done with them, and how he had opened a door of faith for the Gentiles. Acts 14:27

when we are
tempted to cling
to our money,
   unclasp our fingers
   so our abundance
   spills into the world;
when we
turn the keys
in the locks
of our hearts,

    prop the doors open
    with your love so
    anyone can come in;
when we
are filled with
foolish fears and
prattling prejudices,
    unclog our hearts
    so your grace
    may flow more
  freely.

Thursday

For they flatter themselves in
    their own eyes, Psalm 36:2a

carefully
    covering each wrinkle,
  combing the gel
  into my hair to
  cover the grey,
    putting the drops
    in my eyes to
      remove the redness,
my image of
  success,
    youth,
    power,
stares back at me
with fond approval;
but reflected
    in your scarred
  heart, i see myself
      for who i
    truly am, your
beloved
flaws and all.

Friday

He said to her, "Daughter, your faith has made you well; go in peace, and be healed of your disease." Mark 5:34

when her
    religion

would not allow
  her to go to the place
    of wholeness and hope,
the Holy One of healing
came to her,
      so her faith
    could make her
    well.

Saturday

On the sabbath he began to teach in the synagogue, and many who heard him were astounded. They said, "Where did this man get all this? What is this wisdom that has been given to him? What deeds of power are being done by his hands!" Mark 6:2

thinking you
    only
  an unskilled
  laborer with
    callused hands,

we are not
    smart enough
    to realize
  you can repair
    every crack
    in our
  hearts.

Week following Sunday between July 24 and 30 inclusive

Sunday

"Then they also will answer, 'Lord, when was it that we saw you hungry or thirsty or a stranger or naked or sick or in prison, and did not take care of you?'" Matthew 25:44

when?
every second
  every day,
    every person,
  every chance,
but we are
too busy admiring

ourselves
to notice.
when, indeed!

Monday

Steadfast love and
faithfulness will meet;
righteousness and peace
will kiss each other. Psalm 85:10

as justice and
 peace
 speak their vows
 and exchange
 rings,
we join
 hands with
 faithfulness and
 never-ending love,
 dancing the night
 away at the
 reception
 held under the

 stars.

Tuesday

During the night Paul had a vision: there stood a man of Macedonia
pleading with him and saying, "Come over to Macedonia and help
us." When he had seen the vision, we immediately tried to cross
over to Macedonia, being convinced that God had called us to
proclaim the good news to them. Acts 16:9-10

truth be told, Lord?

immediately
 is not often
 found
 in our vocabulary
when another
asks for

 help . . .

Wednesday

When he saw that they were straining at the oars against an adverse wind, he came towards them early in the morning, walking on the sea. He intended to pass them by. Mark 6:48

more astonishing
    than your ability
    to walk on
        water?

your willingness
to step into
our lives
    and face our
    fears with us.

Thursday

And he said, "It is what comes out of a person that defiles."
Mark 7:20

like toothpaste
  from a tube,
those words
    spilling
  from our mouths,
that bitterness
    squeezed
  from our hearts,
the lust
    flowing
  from our eyes
  and minds

can never be
put back.

Friday

Be gracious to me, O LORD,
    for I am languishing;
  O LORD, heal me, for my
    bones are shaking with
    terror. Psalm 6:2

when i
cower
   in bed,
  my knees knocking
  loud enough to
  wake neighbors a
      mile away,
you crawl under
the covers
   with me,
  flashlight in hand,
to take away my
    fears
  with your stories
  and songs.

Saturday

*My soul is satisfied with a
   rich feast,* Psalm 63:5a

with songbirds
    early in the
  morning as
   appetizers;
a dash through
   the sprinklers
  with the dog
  for the soup
    course;
the laughter and
   gentle gibes
  of family and
  friends the
    entree;
and grandchildren
   on our laps
  demanding one more
  story as
     dessert,
our souls are
   indeed

   full!

Week following Sunday between July 31 and August 6 inclusive

Sunday

David danced before the LORD with all his might; 2 Samuel 6:14a

we could be
twirling around
    life with God
    in wonder and delight,

but
  we'd rather lean
    against the wall,
  murmuring under our breath
    about the music chosen,
  the quality of the
    refreshments,
  the band leader.

Monday

How long will you assail a
    person,
  will you batter your victim.
    all of you,
  as you would a leaning
    wall, a tottering fence? Psalm 62:3

the little boy
    teased at the
    school bus stop
  for his hand-me-downs;
the elderly lady
  pushed aside
  in the grocery lane;
the couple
    down the street
    who cannot maintain
  their house, as
  the local council
    prepares to
    cite them;
the family shunned
    simply because
    they come from
  somewhere else . . .

how long
will we just
go along?

Tuesday

He took the blind man by the hand and led him out of the village; and when he had put saliva on his eyes and laid his hands on him, he asked him, "Can you see anything?" And the man looked up and said, "I can see people, but they look like trees, walking."
Mark 8:23-24

we see
    workers, but
  they look like
  illegals stealing
      our jobs;
we see
    teenagers, but
  they look like
  a gang who
  want our money;
we see
    some white-haired
    ladies, but
  they look like
  dandelion puffballs
     about to blow away;
clear our vision,
so we can see people
for who they truly are.

Wednesday

He entered the synagogue and for three months spoke out boldly, and argued persuasively about the kingdom of God. Acts 19:8

i can nitpick
  any opposing view
  and leave it writhing
    on the floor;
i can bluster
    and fluster
  with the best
  during the never-ending
    political season;

i can wake up
> ready to rebut
> the last words
> my spouse spoke
> before we turned
>   out the lights . . .
but
passionately
promote the
> kingdom?

Thursday

I love the LORD, because he
> *has heard*
> *my voice and my*
> *supplications.*
Because he inclined his ear
> *to me,*
> *therefore I will call on him*
> *as long as I live.* Psalm 116:1-2

we sit down,
across from each
other, and after the
server takes the drinks order,
you simply ask,
> 'how are you . . .?'

and two hours
later (after the lunch,
> the laughter,
>   the shared chocolate treat),
i realize
> (again!)
what
a good listener you are
> (though you speak
>   hardly a word)

and why i
love
you
so much.

Friday

Nathan said to David, "You are the man!" 2 Samuel 12:7a

when we
ask why
    some**one**
doesn't shelter
the homeless;
when we
complain that
    no **one**
cares about
kids in poverty;
when we
bemoan the fact that
    every**one**'s
carbon footprint
grows larger with
every step we take;
when we
question why
    any **one**
would be foolish enough
to challenge injustice,
you sadly gaze at us,
whispering,
'you are the
    ones.'

Saturday

Then he took a little child and put it among them; and taking it in his arms, he said to them, "Whoever welcomes one such child in my name welcomes me, and whoever welcomes me welcomes not me but the one who sent me." Mark 9:36-37

they open the
    circle to include
  the kid who has
  come on the last
    night of Bible school;
they try new
    things
  with open arms,
    jumping feet first into

    new songs, stories, play,
      and
  then ask for more;
they take no
    notice of
  another's skin tone,
  accent, or dress;
they hug each
    other as if
  they will never
  see them again
    (or at least
    until tomorrow!);
no wonder
they should
be our role
    models!

Week following Sunday between Aug. 7 and 13 inclusive

Sunday

"He who has the bride is the bridegroom. The friend of the bridegroom, who stands and hears him, rejoices greatly at the bridegroom's voice. For this reason my joy has been fulfilled. He must increase, but I must decrease." John 3:29-30

remind us
of our calling:
  to walk beside you,
    not ahead;
  to rejoice at your words,
    not focus on ours;
  to listen to your heart,
    even as ours break;
  to offer a toast,
    not a rebuke;
  to step aside so
    others can see you.

Monday

"I did not shrink from doing anything helpful, proclaiming the message to you and teaching you publicly and from house to house." Acts 20:20

not striving to be pure and
blameless, but willing

  to dig wells
    for the thirsty;
  to plaster walls
    in crumbling neighborhoods;
  to roll up our sleeves
    and donate blood;
  to jump in puddles
    with silly kids and
    bouncy dogs;

to do anything and
everything for
  anyone and
  everyone.

Tuesday

But when Jesus saw this, he was indignant and said to them, "Let the little children come to me; do not stop them; for it is to such as these that the kingdom of God belongs." Mark 10:14

we spend
  money,
    time
  energy,
trying to keep
the poor,
    broken,
    lonely,
    ostracized,
  away,

never noticing
you reach around
  our rigidity
to draw others
into your grace.

Wednesday

The disciples were perplexed at these words. But Jesus said to them again, "Children, how hard it is to enter the kingdom of God!" Mark 10:24

convinced we have
to make it even
    harder,
we go around
  soldering bars over
    the windows;

  installing thick,
    steel doors;

  upgrading the
    security systems
    of the kingdom,

never hearing the
irony of the words
of the One who
    came to
point to God's

wide-open heart.

Thursday

They were on the road, going up to Jerusalem, and Jesus was walking ahead of them; they were amazed, and those who followed were afraid. Mark 10:32

as you walk
  ahead of us
  towards the
    hate,
   violence,
    prejudice
that would rip us
on the way to
    love,
    inclusion,
    community,
help us to toss
our fears into
  the bins you
  place by the
side of the road.

Friday

They came to Jericho. As he and his disciples and a large crowd were leaving Jericho, Bartimaeus son of Timaeus, a blind beggar, was sitting by the roadside. When he heard that it was Jesus of Nazareth, he began to shout out and say, "Jesus, Son of David, have mercy on me!" Mark 10:46-47

let us not
  ignore the cries
of poverty's children,
    or drive past
  them on our way
  to privilege, but
turn, listening
to their hearts,
    as they open
    our cataracted eyes
to their love.

Saturday

"If anyone says to you, 'Why are you doing this?' just say this, 'The Lord needs it and will send it back here immediately.'" Mark 11:3

when someone asks
      why
  you fly a rainbow
    flag,
  advocate for the
    powerless,
  decrease your carbon
    footprint,
  stand up to
    bullies,
  welcome refugees
    with open arms,
simply say,
  'Jesus needs it'

Week following Sunday between Aug. 14 and 20 inclusive

Sunday

For this reason, those who believe are blessed with Abraham who believed. Galatians 3: 9

we believe in hope,
  but keep despair
  in our back pockets;
we believe in tolerance,
  but take umbrage
  at the words of others;
we believe in love,
  but boil with anger
  at a moment's notice;

we believe
   so
help our unbelief.

Monday

"Wherever you stand praying, forgive, if you have anything against anyone; so that your Father in heaven may also forgive you your trespasses." Mark 11:25

before we
   hand you
  our grocery list
  of expectations and
    wishes,
help us to
  set aside all of
the grudges and
  slights we
carry around, so
there is room
  for your grace
  in our lives.

Tuesday

Do not put your trust in
    princes,
in mortals, in whom there
    is no help. Psalm 146:3

since
we find it so
   easy
  to trust in the

    shallow souls
      of celebrities and
   broken words of
   politicians,

is it any
       wonder
we don't listen to
you?

Wednesday

O LORD, who may abide in
       your tent?
  Who may dwell on your
      holy hill?
[those]
who do not lend money at
      interest,
  and do not take a bribe
      against the innocent.
Those who do these things
      shall never be moved. Psalm 15:1, 5

you throw wide
   the door
  of the kingdom
   to those who
  are more generous
   than cautious,
who say no
   to the lobbyists
   whose clients would put
more families under
   a bridge,
more children scrounging
   dumpsters,
more disabled scrambling
   for services.

Thursday

Turn again, O God of hosts;
  look down from heaven,
      and see; Psalm 80:14a

while others
    pull
  up every
foolishness,
  mistake,
hurtful word,
    backs-turned-to-folks
    reaching out
        to us,
watching over and over
on their devices,
  you notice
the hug offered
  to a co-worker
  just downsized,
the smile shared
  with the teen
  at the café,
the listening ear
  to the lonely gran.

Friday

And as he discussed justice, self-control, and the coming judgment, Felix became frightened and said, "Go away for the present; when I have an opportunity, I will send for you." Acts 24:25

uncomfortable with
    injustice's gaunt stare;
finding it easier to do
    what we want;
and not caring a flip
    about the future,
we hope you
    will go away
  until a more convenient time,

so

continue to speak
your heart
  until we
  pay
attention.

Saturday

"But the one who endures to the end will be saved." Mark 13:13b

faith –

not a
sprint

nor a
marathon

but simply
a daily
walk

with grace.

Week following Sunday between Aug. 21 and 27 inclusive

Sunday

There is no longer Jew or Greek, there is no longer slave or free, there is no longer male and female; for all of you are one in Christ Jesus. Galatians 3:28

you come
    along,
peeling off
the labels and
bar codes
we have stuck on
   others,

so we can see
their true worth
and
identity.

Monday

*The LORD is near to all who
    call on him,
to all who call on him in
    truth.* Psalm 145:18

like a kitten
spooning next
to us,
  purring contentedly
  through the night,

God
is always
near.

Tuesday

"But about that day or hour no one knows, neither the angels in heaven, nor the Son, but only the Father." Mark 13:32

instead
of worrying so much
about when time
will end

may we
focus
on the hour
we are given
now

in which
to serve your
people.

Wednesday

"And now, O LORD my God, you have made your servant king in place of my father David, although I am only a little child; I do not know how to go out or come in." I Kings 3:7

when we do not
  know how
to go out,
you pave the
    way
  with your grace
  so we may find
  your heart;

when we do not
  know how
to come in,
you throw wide
     the door,
  gather us up
  in your arms,
and carry us
to your rocking chair
where we snuggle
in your lap, falling asleep
listening to the gentle
beating of your heart.

Thursday

"and wherever he enters, say to the owner of the house, 'The Teacher asks, Where is my guest room where I may eat the Passover with my disciples?' He will show you a large room upstairs, furnished and ready. Make preparations for us there."
Mark 14:14-15

may my heart
be a guest room,
  furnished and ready
  to embrace your love,
as it wanders
the lonely streets
  of our lives;
may my mind
become a guest room,
  where your words
  will be welcomed
and transformed
into compassion
which welcomes
everyone i meet;
may my soul
offer a guest room
  where your justice
   may recuperate
and then lead me
by the hand
to every corner
where oppression
sells its deadly wares.

Friday

Now I know that the LORD
 will help his anointed; Psalm 20:6a

now,

in the woman
 patiently
 teaching her grandson
 how to drive;

in the doctor
 pacing the hallways
 as he figures out
 the best treatment
 for the child's cancer;

in the father
 who heads off
 to his second job,
 carrying weariness
 deep in his bones
 from the first . . .

i know.

Saturday

"Let it be known to you then that this salvation of God has been sent to the Gentiles; they will listen." Acts 28:28

while
the insiders
always hear
the gospel

it is
the outsiders
who listen
and
live it out.

Week following Sunday between Aug. 28 and Sept. 3 inclusive

Sunday

Do not neglect the gift that is in you, 1 Timothy 4:14a

we are
so focused
on the gift/s
  we do not
  have
we miss using
the one/s
we do

Monday

. . . mercy triumphs over justice. James 2:13b

when we could
receive what we
deserve,
  you shower us
  with what we never
  expect;

when the door
could be slammed
in our faces,
  you open your
  heart to us;

when we could
spend our lives
alone and broken,
  you offer eternity
  with you;

may our mercy
towards others
be at least a drop
of that ocean
you dip us in.

Tuesday

What good is it, my brothers and sisters, if you say you have faith but do not have works? Can faith save you? James 2:14

what good is it
if we pray
but do not
practice,

if we listen
but do not
love,

if we give
but still hoard
grudges,

if we believe
but do
nothing?

Wednesday

*Say among the nations, "The
    LORD is king!
  The world is firmly
    established; it shall
    never be moved.
He will judge the peoples
    with equity."* Psalm 96:10

not with favoritism
    or false promises,
not with anger
    or fiery flames,
not with punishment
    or pain;
not with a
   well-creased list
   in your pocket,
or a grudge
   lodged deep
   in your heart;

but fairness
will be your
measuring stick
and that is all
we need.

Thursday

Who is wise and understanding among you? Show by your good life that your works are done with gentleness born of wisdom.
James 3:13

in
the little girl
who invites
  the shunned boy
  to her party,

the families
who open their homes
  to refugees
  turned away
  by nation after nation,

the lifer
who fosters
a dog
  to companion
  a man
  she will never meet,

we meet the
wise ones
of our age.

Friday

Do not remember the sins of
    my youth or my
    transgressions; Psalm 25:7a

the roller-skating
around sin's rink
  that skinned my knees;

jumping off faith's edge
and breaking my leg
  because pride
  double-dared me;

my battering words
that bruised your

heart over and over,
all have been
    tossed into
your crystal sea
of forgetfulness.

Saturday

At three o'clock Jesus cried out with a loud voice, "Eloi, Eloi, lema sabachthani?" which means, "My God, my God, why have you forsaken me?" Mark 15:34

Holy One,

when we arrive
on the other side
of our despair,

may we find
you
in your fields
of
hope.

Week following Sunday between Sept. 4 and 10 inclusive

Sunday

But Peter and John answered them, "Whether it is right in God's sight to listen to you rather than to God, you must judge; for we cannot keep from speaking about what we have seen and heard." Acts 4:19-20

we see the homeless
    veterans
  huddled in the doorways,
    and tighten our earbuds;
we watch the bully
  on the playground
  through the car window,
    and turn the radio up;
we notice the bruises
  on the secretary
  in the office, and
    ask 'what's next on the agenda?'

have mercy on us,
for finding it so easy
to keep from speaking.

Monday

O LORD, in the morning you
 hear my voice;
 in the morning I plead my
  case to you, and watch. Psalm 5:3

i watch
the news
 and avert my eyes
 from the horrifying
  image of the little
  body on the beach;

i observe
the tent city
 down by the banks
 of the river, as
 i hurry to the
 expensive game
  at the stadium;

i notice
the parents
 lined up to
 enter the food
 pantry first
 thing in the
 morning,
after my breakfast
meeting at the
all-u-can-eat buffet;

help me to see,
Lord,
 through your eyes
 of compassion and
  hope,
 as you plead
 your case for

justice.

Tuesday

And as if it had been a light thing for him to walk in the sins of Jeroboam son of Nebat, 1 Kings 16:31a

because
our sins seem
　as light
　as a feather,

we find
it easy to believe
　they will never
　weigh us down.

Wednesday

make my joy complete: be of the same mind, having the same love, being in full accord and of one mind. Philippians 2:2

be of the same
　　　mind,
　but don't expect
　everyone to agree with
　　　you;

have the same
　　　love,
　yet share it
　in a variety of
　　　ways;

be of one
　　　accord,
　yet celebrate
　the diversity of
　　　gifts;

be of one
　　　mind,
　but learn from
　each other's
　　　wisdom.

Thursday

But even if I am being poured out as a libation over the sacrifice and the offering of your faith, I am glad and rejoice with all of you -- Philippians 2:17

perhaps
death
is the final
act
of worship
we offer to
God.

Friday

Yet whatever gains I had, these I have come to regard as loss because of Christ. Philippians 3:7

how easily
we boast
   about
  dumping all
  the garbage
    of our lives,
but how loudly
we grumble
   over
  giving up
  all that
  we think
is of value.

Saturday

Brothers and sisters, join in imitating me, and observe those who live according to the example you have in us. Philippians 3:17

not by grandstand
    plays
  or grandiose
    schemes;
not by bombastic
    bromides
  or pious
    platitudes;

but simply
  by watching,
    by listening,
  by mirroring
those who know
you best
do we live
as you hope.

Week following Sunday between Sept. 11 and 17 inclusive

Sunday

Who is like the LORD our
    God,
  who is seated on high,
who looks far down
  on the heavens and the
    earth? Psalm 113: 5-6

shading your eyes
  with callused hands,
  you stare like a dog
  intent on the food
  on the counter, until
spying us, no bigger than
a dot on the horizon,
  you put down creation
  and rush to scoop us up
in your love.

Monday

For you, O LORD, are most
    high over all the earth;
  you are exalted far above
    all gods. Psalm 97:9

in the bright
  morning star
  pointing the way
  on my morning walk;
in the geese
  fleeting across
  the autumn sky;

in the multi-colored
  leaves
    tumbling across
    the lawns;
in the cool
  breeze which
    awakens a
    slumbering kitten;

you are exalted
by all creation.

Tuesday

From that time Jesus began to proclaim, "Repent, for the kingdom of heaven has come near." Matthew 4:17

when we turn
from building fences
and camps,
to embrace
the refugees
with open arms;

when we turn
away from our
prejudiced fears,
to fulfill
the long-denied dreams
of our sisters and brothers;

when we turn
from bullying those
clearing the banquet tables,
to take them
by the hand
to the place of honor,

we will see how
near we are
to your kingdom.

Wednesday

But we speak God's wisdom, secret and hidden, which God decreed before the ages for our glory. 1 Corinthians 2:7

in the dog
who knows exactly
which person at the
    rehab center
needs her compassionate
presence the most;

in the Spirit's
exuberant gusts which
snap us out of
    our fears,
as well as her
gentle caress
which dries the tears
  on our cheeks;

in the little child
whose simple
    innocence
challenges our
complicated analyses,

we discover your
    wisdom
which we too
often fail to
notice.

Thursday

When Jesus saw the crowds, he went up the mountain; and after he sat down, his disciples came to him. Then he began to speak, and taught them, saying: Matthew 5:1-2

blessed are

those who fill their emptiness with God's hope;
   those who mingle their tears with others;
those who care for creation;
   those who fill the hungry and thirsty;
those who show mercy when others show their backs;
   those who see God in imperfect people;
the children who play in peace, not at war;
   the refugees, who carry the kingdom of heaven to us.

Friday

*You are a hiding place for
  me;
 you preserve me from
  trouble;
 you surround me with glad
  cries of deliverance.* Psalm 32:7

when the taunts
   of others torment
  me,
       i am soothed
       by your encompassing
       silence;
when i am
   battered about
   by anger and hurt,
  i can crawl
  in your lap and
       be cradled
       in your grace;
when my fears
scuttle about under
the bed,
     you turn on
     your flashlight
   so we can make
    shadow puppets
       on the wall,
     until i fall asleep,
my fingers entwined
with yours.

Saturday

*You have kept count of my
    tossings;
  put my tears in your
    bottle.
  Are they not in your
    record?* Psalm 56:8

contrary to
    expectations,
the book opened

on your lap as
you sit in your
rocker late at
  night, is not
filled with our
    failings, but our fears;
while sipping
the mug of tea
brewed from our tears,
you write down
all the things
that keep us awake
  through the night,
and engrave them
on your heart.

Week following Sunday between Sept. 18 and 24 inclusive

Sunday

*There is a river whose
    streams make glad the
    city of God,
  the holy habitation of the
    Most High. Psalm 46:4*

the folks who
   open their homes
  to refugees
  fleeing unspeakable
      horrors;
the little girl
who empties her
piggy bank to
   sponsor a well
   in a village
  she will never
      visit;
the retiree
  who stays with
  local families
  rather than at
  five-star venues
     whenever she
     travels overseas:

drop
    by   drop,
justice carves a
river through
the granite heart
of the world.

Monday

We are fools for the sake of Christ, 1 Corinthians 4:10a

after helping us
put on the greasepaint,
  with the blue stars under
        our eyes,
  and the yellow teardrops
  at the corner of
        our mouths,
you hand us
the baggy pants
and wide red suspenders,
  the polka-dotted shirt,
  the frizzy, rainbow wig,
  the big red nose and
    shoes that are
    10x too big,
whispering,
'this is the uniform
for the day (
  and every day
)

Tuesday

Mighty King, lover of
    justice,
  you have established
    equity;
you have executed justice
  and righteousness in
    Jacob. Psalm 99:4

through
    weakness,
  you strengthen us
  to help others;

through
    suffering,
  you knit together
  our brokenness;

through
    abhorring injustice,
  you teach us
  to love the
    oppressed;

you reign
over us
    simply
by serving

    us

Wednesday

As the mountains surround
    Jerusalem,
  so the LORD surrounds his
    people,
  from this time on and
    forevermore. Psalm 125:2

as a daughter
    places a shawl
  around the shoulders
  of her dozing mother;
as a father
    puts another blanket
  over his sleeping child
  on a winter night;
as a sister
    hugs her little
      brother
  after he misses
  the wide open goal,
so you calm
    us
  in every moment
    with every grace.

Thursday

"All things are lawful for me," but not all things are beneficial. "All things are lawful for me," but I will not be dominated by anything.
1 Corinthians 6:12

if all the vices
  do it so
    easily,
why do i
have so much
    trouble
  being dominated
  by
    grace,
      hope,
    peace,
      wonder,
    gentleness,
and so many more
such gifts?

Friday

O LORD, do not rebuke me in
    your anger,
  or discipline me in your
    wrath. Psalm 6:1

no slap on
  the cheek,
  but a gentle
    kiss;
no harsh words
  of correction,
  but whispers
    of grace;
no time-out
  chair in the corner,
  but a comfy
    lap;
no remembrance
  of past foolishness,
  but a glimpse
    of that future
    together;

in than giving
me more than i
      deserve,
  you offer
  just what
    i need.

Saturday

My soul clings to you;
  your right hand upholds
     me. Psalm 63:8

when stress
thunders through me,
  i can run
  to your room,
     and snuggle
     under the covers
    with you;
when fear
roots
    me in place,
  you take me
  by the hand,
     whispering,
'let's cross over
to the other side,
    where hope
    is waiting
  with a cup
  of tea.'

Week following Sunday between Sept. 25 and Oct. 1 inclusive

Sunday

he restores my soul. Psalm 23:5a

when
i wander
    so far
  from you, even
    the gps doesn't know
    where i am,

you
turn to
bring me
    back into
  your
heart's fold.

Monday

But as for me, my feet had
    almost stumbled;
my steps had nearly
    slipped.   Psalm 73:2

you pick me
  up,
wash off my
  bruised knees,
bandage my
  scraped elbows,
tighten my
  helmet, and
putting me
  upright on my
  training-wheeled
    life, you
   give me a
   push, with
  an encouraging,
'keep pedaling,
you'll get it!'

Tuesday

"Is there anyone among you who, if your child asks for bread,
will give a stone? Or if the child asks for a fish, will give a snake?"
Matthew 7:9-10

you're kidding,
    right?
i'll do anything
  and everything
  to make sure
  my kids get
   three squares
   a day,

    and a safe
        place
   to live and
   play without
      any worries
      or fears;
but those other
  children
 of yours . . .

someone has
to eat the stones
and play with the snakes,
     right?

Wednesday

"Not everyone who says to me, 'Lord, Lord,' will enter the kingdom of heaven, but only the one who does the will of my Father in heaven."
Matthew 7:21

if

we embrace
    justice
  more than
   our prejudices;
when
we make that
    hard choice to
  love, though
     hatred is
    easier to grasp;
should
we choose
to whisper
    hope
  rather than
  shout despair,

what do we
have to fear
when time
comes to an
    end?

Thursday

*The LORD protects the
    simple;* Psalm 116:6a

joy -
  not the convolutions
  of a preacher, but
      the giggles
      of kids in the tub;

wonder -
  not the general
  theory of relativity, but
      a dog leaping
      high to snatch
      a ball out of the air;

hope -
  not a thick
  theological tome, but
      a mother
      cradling her
      feverish child;

how we complicate
your simple gifts!

Friday

*and there was a leper who came to him and knelt before him, saying,
"Lord, if you choose, you can make me clean."* Matthew 8:2

i could
    raise a child
    out of poverty, or
  just keep accumulating
  more stuff;

i could
    help clean up
    the environment, or
  keep on clomping around
  in my carbon-laden boots;

i could
> welcome a
> refugee family, or
build barriers
to keep them out;

Lord,
help me to
> choose!

Saturday

Satisfy us in the morning
> *with your steadfast*
> *love,*
so that we may rejoice and
> *be glad all our days.* Psalm 90:14

in the gentle
> rain
which washes
us with your
> grace;
in the October
> moon
which watches
over us as
we sleep
> in your
> peace;
in the softly falling
> snow
which wraps
us in your
> compassion;
in the creeping
> sunrise
which nudges
us out of bed
> as we slip
> our feet into your
> hope,

we rejoice.

Week following Sunday between Oct. 2 and 8 inclusive

Sunday

*Let everything that breathes
    praise the LORD!
Praise the LORD!* Psalm 150:6

kittens purring
  in winter's
  sunbeam;
dogs snuffling
  in the leaves
  for squirrels;

babies cooing
  in their cribs
  each morning;
seniors huffing
  on their morning
  walks;

kids hyperventilating
  before a
  date;

let all
praise the Lord!

Monday

Do not seek your own advantage, but that of the other.
1 Corinthians 10:24

when i could
be at the head
    table, let me
  offer the seat
  to the dishwasher
  in the kitchen;
when i
hunger for
    the world's
    accolades, let me
  hear the cries
  of the outcasts;

when i could
run the whole
    circus, let me
  wield the shovel
and broom
  behind the elephants.

Tuesday

My soul thirsts for God,
  for the living God.
When shall I come and
    behold
  the face of God? Psalm 42:2

the radiant
    smile
  of a child
running into
her grandma's
    arms
  at the airport;

the wearied
    eyes
  of the nurse
  keeping watch
    in the long night;

the laugh lines
framing mom's
    mouth
  as she reads
  to the children
  at the library;

the frown on dad's
    forehead
  as he struggles
  to explain algebra
    to his daughter:

your face
is all around me . . .

Wednesday

Happy are those
  who do not follow the
    advice of the wicked,
or take the path that sinners
    tread,
  or sit in the seat of
    scoffers; Psalm 1:1

when i
would heed
   the nitpickers,
  let me listen
  to the songs
    of little children;

when i
would sneak down
   seduction's back alleys,
  let me find
  the grace-bordered
    paths
   to the kingdom;

when i
would hunger for
   power's throne,
  let me crawl
  into your lap
    and listen
  to your heart.

Thursday

in your right hand are
    pleasures forevermore. Psalm 16:11c

when the world
would run a
     long con
    on us,
  gaffling
    every hope
    we have;

when the evil one
puts healing
        under one of
        the shells, shuffling
    them around, and
    then challenging us
    to make the right choice,

you simply open
your hand (filled
    with grace, wonder,
    peace, joy, reconciliation,
    and o, so much more),
  saying, 'take
  what you need, there's
    enough for everyone.'

Friday

On the contrary, the members of the body that seem to be weaker are indispensable, 1 Corinthians 12:22

the teenager
    with wisdom
  beyond his
        tears;

the rough sleeper
    who saved
    her unit in
  the war;

the actress
    with blades
  auditioning
    for the role of Eliza Doolittle;

the asylum seeker
    with a PhD
    in persistence:

these are the
    missing parts
  of that puzzle
  we call family.

Saturday

Now you are the body of Christ and individually members of it.
1 Corinthians 12:27

    foolish and infallible,
    pretentious and pitiful,
    honored and humbled,
    broken and healed:
you are the body of Christ;

    bread which can feed
        those hungering for hope,
    a cup which refreshes
        those thirsting for justice,
    a table with room
        enough to welcome all:
this is the body of Christ;

    in shadowed corners
        and at busy crossroads,
    on playing fields
        and in hospice rooms,
    challenging power's presumptions
        and easing the burdens
        of the overlooked:
be the body of Christ . . .

Week following Sunday between Oct. 9 and 15 inclusive

Sunday

Let the words of my mouth
    and the meditation of
      my heart
be acceptable to you,
O LORD, my rock and my
    redeemer. Psalm 19:14

may my words
    heal others, not
        break them;
    share hope, not
        hoard it;
    lift lives, not
        push them down;

   welcome all, not
      reject them,
as i delve deeply
into the ruminations
of your heart.

Monday

Love is patient; love is kind; love is not envious or boastful or arrogant or rude. It does not insist on its own way; it is not irritable or resentful; it does not rejoice in wrongdoing, but rejoices in the truth. It bears all things, believes all things, hopes all things, endures all things. Love never ends. 1 Corinthians 13:4-8a

love
waits in the rain
  for the straggling child
  jumping in every puddle;
offers a hand
  to the one
  who gave a slap;
refuses to give
  in to
  grudges;
celebrates the frankness
  of those who
  discomfort it;
it gives birth to grace,
counts on the good in every person,
takes heart in every moment,
bests the worst it is offered;

love never gives up.

Tuesday

But neither he nor his servants nor the people of the land listened to the words of the LORD that he spoke through the prophet Jeremiah. Jeremiah 37:2

in the teenager
    speaking before her
    church's council
  in support of
  housing immigrants;

in the woman
    wheeling her chair
  in the marathon
  to raise money
  for children with
    disabilities;
in the donor
    saying a prayer
  for the person
  they will never meet,
    but whose life
    will be extended
  by the organ donation,

prophets are
all around us.

Wednesday

Answer me when I call,
    O God of my right!
  You gave me room when I
    was in distress.
  Be gracious to me, and
    hear my prayer. Psalm 4:1

when i volunteer
    at an affordable
    housing site, foregoing
  that resort vacation;
when i stock
    the shelves at
    the food pantry, instead
  of feasting at the
  5-star restaurant;
when i become
    a voice for those
    who always seem
  to be just out
  of power's earshot,
i join you,
God of justice,
  in answering
  the prayers of
those in distress.

Thursday

Do not let the foot of the
  arrogant tread on me,
or the hand of the wicked
  drive me away. Psalm 36:11

when the
  highfalutins
  stick out their
  feet to trip me
    on the way
    to sit with the
      vulnerable,
  show me how
  to jump over;

when the
    rogues
  would put their
  hands on my chest
  to keep me from
    helping the hopeless,
  let me look
  them in the eye,
    inviting, 'why
    not join us?'

Friday

Now I would remind you, brothers and sisters, of the good news that I proclaimed to you, which you in turn received, in which also you stand, through which also you are being saved, if you hold firmly to the message that I proclaimed to you--unless you have come to believe in vain. 1 Corinthians 15:1-2

in the bus driver
    who guides
    the kid through
  the intricacies of
      algebra;
in the store clerk
    spending her
    time off learning
    a second language

     to communicate
     with customers;
in the barista
    offering a shoulder
    to the grief-stricken
    regular who still
    misses her husband,

the gospel
is still
proclaimed.

Saturday

But in fact Christ has been raised from the dead, the first fruits of those who have died. 1 Corinthians 15:20

when our words
    are gracious and calm,
  not bitter and uncaring,
    we share the facts of hope with others;
when we stop to pick up
    all those we have
  knocked over in our hasty fear,
    we practice resurrection love;
when we offer peace
    instead of picking up weapons,
  we turn our neighborhoods
    into farmers markets of your first fruits.

Week following Sunday between Oct. 16 and 22 inclusive

Sunday

During the night Paul had a vision: there stood a man of Macedonia pleading with him and saying, "Come over to Macedonia and help us." When he had seen the vision, we immediately tried to cross over to Macedonia, being convinced that God had called us to proclaim the good news to them. Acts 16:9-10

(far too) often,
    we stand on
    the corner, thinking
  we have to wait
  for the signal to change to
    Walk

before we dare
to take hope, grace,
peace, and life
to those who are
waving their emptiness
at us on the
other side.

Monday

He chose our heritage for us,
the pride of Jacob whom
he loves. Psalm 47:4

peace
    not power;
hope,
    not hatred;
kindness,
    not killing;
grace,
    not crudeness;
justice,
    not oppression;
generosity,
    not greed,
these are our
  heirlooms.

Tuesday

among all her lovers she has no one to comfort her . . . with none to
comfort her. Lamentations 1:2b, 9c

a shot in the arm
    for the weak;
alleviating the loneliness
    of the widowed;
deferring to the
    disadvantaged;
consoling those hearts
    ravaged by rage;
supporting the forgotten
    left by the side
    of the economic road . . .

help us to be
the comfort
others need.

Wednesday

"So it is lawful to do good on the sabbath." Matthew 12:12b

sadly,
we seem to
  believe (and
     act)
as if we
can do good
on the Sabbath
    only.

Thursday

I am the LORD your God,
  who brought you up out of
    the land of Egypt,
  Open your mouth wide and
    I will fill it. Psalm 81:10

let us

open our mouths
  so that you
  may fill them
with words of
  comfort for
  the grieving;

open our ears
  so that you
  may fill them
with the cries
  of the hungry;

open our hearts
  so that you
  may fill them
with that compassion
  for the forgotten;

open our souls
   so that you
   may fill them
 with
      you.

Friday

Let all that you do be done in love. 1 Corinthians 16:14

of course
i can donate
   some canned goods
   to a food bank
 in
   making space for
   more in my pantry;

i can encourage
   others to house
   refugee families
 in
   dealing with
   my fears of
   them moving into
   my neighborhood;

i can hope
   the free clinic
   manages to keep
   its doors open
 in
   gu lt for the
   health care benefits
   i enjoy because
   i am so well off;

but do all these things
     (and more)
  in   love?

Saturday

"I tell you, on the day of judgment you will have to give an account for every careless word you utter;" Matthew 12:36

i trust
    that on
  the day of
    judgment,
the only
     Word
  that counts
  will be
grace.

Week following Sunday between Oct. 23 and 29 inclusive

Sunday

But wanting to justify himself, he asked Jesus, "And who is my neighbor?" Luke 10:29

the woman
    sitting next
  to the empty
     rocking chair
  on her front porch;

the immigrant
    trying to figure
    out the intricacies
of a car engine, so
    he can get
    to his two jobs;

the transgendered
    student
  shunned by peers
    at the local
    school . . .

my neighbors
are all around
me.

Monday

*For God alone my soul waits in
    silence;
  from him comes my
    salvation.* Psalm 62:1

i will
leave my
    mobile
  off;

i will
power down my
    PC;

i will not
pick up my
    remote
  to turn on
  the talking heads;

and in the
    (uncomfortable)
  silence, i
will wait

    for

        you.

Tuesday

and in front of the throne there is something like a sea of glass, like crystal. Revelation 4:6a

you will
    invite us
  to step foot
  onto your sailboat,
where our maimed memories,
      shattered hearts,
    and fractured souls
  will seep out of
  the corners of our eyes, dripping
    down slowly to join
    those of our sisters and brothers
        in that crystal sea

  of your forgetfulness.

Wednesday

Then one of the elders said to me, "Do not weep. See, the Lion of the tribe of Judah, the Root of David, has conquered, so that he can open the scrolls and its seven seals." Then I saw between the throne and the four living creatures and among the elders a Lamb standing as if it had been slaughtered . . . Revelation 5:5-6a

not as
a ravenous,
    lion, roaring
  for its next meal, but
    as a Lamb,
  who searches
  for all the lost
      shepherds,
  until we are
    found,
you come.

Thursday

Return, O my soul, to your
    rest,
  for the LORD has dealt
    bountifully with you. Psalm 116:7

noticing the empty
    space next to you,
  you put your feet
  into the cold slippers,
and wrap yourself
    in the frayed shawl;
finding me before
    the mullioned
  window, staring
  out into life's
     abyss,
you take me
by the hand, and
   lead me back
  to bed, cuddling
  with me until I
  fall asleep in your
embrace.

Friday

*All the paths of the LORD are
steadfast love and
faithfulness,* Psalm 25:10a

using **hesed**
    as your base material,

  you lay out
  your paving stones
                of
    grace
      hope
     wonder
 joy
       peace
   inclusion
     reconciliation,

screeding them together
  with the gritty
  particles of your
      heart,
shaping
   a path

  to your kingdom.

Saturday

*"They will hunger no more,
    and thirst no more;
the sun will not strike
    them,
nor any scorching heat;
for the Lamb at the center of
    the throne will be their
    shepherd,
and he will guide them to
    springs of the water of
    life,
and God will wipe away
    every tear from their
    eyes."* Revelation 7:16-17

a cup of
> water
> for all who
>> thirsted for justice;

a warm
> home
> for all thrown
> out into the
>> cold;

a sumptuous
> feast
> for those who
>> hunger for hope;

tears
> transformed
> into wine;
no tricks,
> just treats,

when we knock
> on your

>> door.

Week following Sunday between Oct. 30 and Nov. 5 inclusive

Sunday

"Instead, strive for his kingdom, and these things will be given to you as well." Luke 12:31

in dog walkers
> and street hawkers,
in those who
> put up with us and
> those who nudge us;
in those who chase
> after you with abandon,
> and those who drag
> their doubts with them;
in the grandfather
> just around the
> corner,

    and the mother
        in a war-torn country,

we find your kingdom
we have been searching for
    in all the wrong places.

Monday

The voice of the LORD
    shakes the wilderness;
the LORD shakes the
    wilderness of Kadesh. Psalm 29:8

when the cries
    of the
  hungry
shatter our
    mealtimes;

when the whispered
    memories
  of the
hospice patients
    break our hearts;

when the hopes
    of
  immigrant parents
  for their children
pierce our prejudices,

the voice of the
    Lord
shakes the wilderness
of our apathy.

Tuesday

These things I remember,
  as I pour out my soul; Psalm 42:4a

how you do
    not give up
    on me, but

```
     come and find
           me
     every time i
       lose my way;
how you love
           me
     when i turn
     my back on
           you,
       and how
     you turn towards
           me
       every time
       i call.
```

Wednesday

Who is left among you that saw this house in its former glory? How does it look to you now? Is it not in your sight as nothing?
Haggai 2:3

```
we look around
               at
       empty pews with
       hymnals turning
                   yellow,
         classrooms filling
         up with dust
                   bunnies,
       parking lots where
       grass grows out the
                   cracks, but
you see
       a sanctuary for
       homeless families;
         rooms being flipped
         into small businesses;
       basketball courts,
       a vegetable market,
       a labyrinth.
nothing?
```

Thursday

Then the LORD replied with gracious and comforting words to the angel who talked with me. Zechariah 1:13

bandages
>   or
> lacerations,
hope
>   or
> despair,
comfort
>   or
> disdain,
grace
>   or
> grumbling;
given the chance,
will I reply with
> weapons
>   or
> words?

Friday

Jesus said to them, "They need not go away; you give them something to eat." Matthew 14:16

when we're
> tempted
> to close the
> drapes, hoping
> the homeless will
> think no one is home;

> to turn out
> the lights so
>   the hungry will
>   think we have
>   left for the day;

> to hop in our
> car and drive off
>   before the busload
>   of refugees arrives;

> to post a sign
> reading 'no compassion
>   available today'
> on the front door,

remind us that
there is no
    need

i/you/we

cannot fill.

Saturday

But immediately Jesus spoke to them and said, "Take heart, it is I; do not be afraid." Matthew 14:27

when we long
  to build higher walls
 (usually nicknamed 'peace')
  to keep all the
  you-know-who out;
when we close
  our eyes, hoping
  our fears will all
    dissipate like
    the morning mist,
you stand on
the other side, reminding,
       "hey, it's only me."

Week following Sunday between Nov. 6 and 12 inclusive

Sunday

"But when you give a banquet, invite the poor, the crippled, the lame, and the blind." Luke 14:13

let us give
   thanks
  in this season,
 by putting another
 leaf in the table, to
  make room for those
  who are always
    serving us (even
 while we quibble over
 their gratuity);
let us find the
   Baby

    this year,
  by affirming
  the giftedness
      of those
        whose lives
  we too often
ignore.

Monday

"It is not what goes into the mouth that defiles a person, but it is what comes out of the mouth that defiles." Matthew 15:11

of all the things
we could speak
out about:
  justice for refugees;
  children in poverty;
  epidemic racism;
  homeless veterans;
  and so much more,
we're going to
spin our time
quibbling about
  who sells the best coffee???

kyrie eleison

Tuesday

She said, "Yes, Lord, yet even the dogs eat the crumbs that fall from their masters' table." Matthew 15:27

with the crumbs
    of hope,
  we could
    restore families;
with the crumbs
    of peace,
  we could
    end wars;
with the crumbs
    of grace,
  we could
    transform urban blight

      into gardens of
        laughter and life,
if we only had
a crumb of
      faith.

Wednesday

Offer right sacrifices,
  and put your trust in the
      LORD. Psalm 4:5

let us make
    justice
  the gift we offer each
    day,
trusting you
to receive
     and multiply
  it.

Thursday

  "to her it has been granted to
     be clothed
  with fine linen, bright and
    pure" --
for the fine linen is the righteous deeds of the saints.
Revelation 19:8

one day,

you will hand us
    that garment
  woven from the threads of
hope we shared,
  joy we poured out,
love we gave away,
  justice we supported,
grace we refused to hoard,
    and
  as we slip it on,
  you will smile,
  clapping your hands,

"a perfect fit!"

Friday

*Do not be like a horse or a
    mule, without
    understanding,
  whose temper must be
    curbed with bit and
    bridle,
  else it will not stay near
    you.* Psalm 32:9

may your
    grace
  be an invisible
    fence
  which keeps our
    anger
  from running away
  and hurting someone
    in its confusion.

Saturday

*in God I trust; I am not
    afraid.
  What can a mere mortal
    do to me?* Psalm 56:11

in the workers
    sweeping up
    the fears,
in the nurses
    whose backs
    ache from the
    weight of tears,
in the grandparents
    comforting children
    whose mother
    will not be coming home,
in the servers
    who suddenly became
    first responders,
in the refugees
    who will become
    scapegoats,

we find you
and trust that
in the jumbled emotions
of anger,
    anxiety,
  vengeance,
      and loss,
  we will find
  your hope,
  your compassion,
  your forgiveness
surrounding us.

Week following Sunday between Nov. 13 and 19 inclusive

Sunday

"You cannot serve God and wealth." Luke 16:13c

tempted to elect
   Mammon
  as leader of the
      country;
making reservations
at Chez Mammon
   3 times a
      day;
putting
   mammon's medallion
  around our necks
     for protection,
remind us
of our calling
to serve you
    as you pour
    your grace
  so abundantly
  into our lives.

Monday

One generation shall laud
   your works to another,
  and shall declare your
    mighty acts. Psalm 145:4

i learned
    forgiveness
   through my mother's
       touch,
   and comfort my children
   with it when
     they mess up;
i found your
    joy in the
    games played
   with my friends, and
   offer it to the
     preschoolers
  as i read to them;
my teacher
    modeled
   your patience
   when i struggled
   with biology, and
    i practice it
    with the teenagers
   who pester me
   with difficult questions;
grace
    wonder
  hope
     love
are not precious jewels
to be placed in
       storage,

   but are to be
  gifted away.

Tuesday

He said to them, "Because of your little faith. For truly I tell you, if you have faith the size of a mustard seed, you will say to this mountain, 'Move from here to there,' and it will move; and nothing will be impossible for you." Matthew 17:20

alternating
   between glancing
    at our watch,

   and peering down
     the road for
     the truck to come
    dump its load
      of faith
   in our lives, we
absentmindedly
    pick up the broom
  to sweep away that
  pesky seed which keeps
    getting stuck
  in the floorboards
of our souls.

Wednesday

you make the gateways of
      the morning and the
         evening shout for joy. Psalm 65:8b

at dawn,
   i awake
  to the sun singing,
  'my Lord, what a morning'
while the stars
   lullaby me to
   sleep each night,
and in every moment
in between, your carols
     of grace and hope
  fill my heart.

Thursday

And the city has no need of sun or moon to shine on it, for the glory of God is its light, and its lamp is the Lamb. The nations will walk by its light, and the kings of the earth will bring their glory into it. Its gates will never be shut by day--and there will be no night there.
Revelation 21:23-25

unlike us,

   your city
   is always
      open
    to anyone

      to come and
          live,

just like your
heart.

Friday

"Take care that you do not despise one of these little ones; for, I tell you, in heaven their angels continually see the face of my Father in heaven." Matthew 18:10

when we park
   in the space
  reserved for the
      disabled (we'll
   only be acoupleofminutes);
when we join
   in the jibes
  about 'slow' Jane
     at work;
when we power up
   our windows
  as the homeless
    veteran
   looks at our car;
when we want
   the borders closed
  out of nothing
  more than fear,
angels
wipe away
   the tears
  streaming down
    your face.

Saturday

*And let everyone who hears
   say, "Come."
And let everyone who is
   thirsty come.
Let anyone who wishes take
   the water of life as a
   gift.* Revelation 22:17

we have
more than enough
    room,
more than enough
    food,
more than enough
    water,
more than enough
    hope,

yet
we continue to say
  'stay'
 to those who
 have so little.

Christ the King or Reign of Christ (Sunday between Nov. 20 and 26) and following

Sunday

Welcome one another, therefore, just as Christ welcomed you, for the glory of God. Romans 15:7

you welcome
   all
 who have
 had every door
  slammed in their
   faces:
poverty's children,
    street walkers,
 cleaners of our hotel bathrooms,
   asylum seekers,
  ebola carriers;

and then,

  you even embrace
     us,
  who seem
  to have difficulty
  opening our hearts
to anyone.

Monday

*Therefore pride is their
    necklace;
  violence covers them like a
    garment.* Psalm 73:6

i could
   put my diamond
   cufflinks in my shirt,
 a solid-gold cross
   around my neck;
 the rings signifying
   victories over others
   on my fingers,
slipping into my
anger-tight jeans
  and bullying jumper,
or
i could go
into the world
as naked
and vulnerable as
you.

Tuesday

Now that you have purified your souls by your obedience to the truth so that you have genuine mutual love, love one another deeply from the heart. 1 Peter 1:22

scraping the edges
    of our hearts
 to gift others
 is easy,
   but that precious
   love which is
 deep down inside?

Wednesday

*"I will abundantly bless its
    provisions;
 I will satisfy its poor with
    bread."* Psalm 132:15

when
    we would feed
  the hungry with
  zero-calorie platitudes,
    you would assuage
    their emptiness
  from our groaning tables,
      offering us
      the leftovers.

Thursday

"Am I not allowed to do what I choose with what belongs to me? Or are you envious because I am generous?" Matthew 20:15

yes,
we are envious
     that
    you find it
    so easy
    to give away
      so much,
  when we struggle
  to even let go
     of our
    pocket change.

Friday

But even if you do suffer for doing what is right, you are blessed. Do not fear what they fear, and do not be intimidated, 1 Peter 3:14

every day
  we are offered
     fear
    worry
      prejudice
    anger
     and hate
at incredibly
      discounted
   prices (they can even
      be put on layaway)
    but not everything
    is the bargain
    we are seeking.

Saturday

Be hospitable to one another without complaining. 1 Peter 4:9

tempted
  to bang the
      oven door
      while others
    take naps;
to mutter under
      our breath
      doing the dishes,
    while the kids
    play soccer in
      the yard;
to stare daggers
      at those watching a game
    while the garbage
    isn't walking itself
      to the bin,
remind us that
      hospitality
  is what our
  hearts do,
not so much our
      bodies.

New Year's Eve or Day

For everything there is a season, and a time for every matter under heaven: Ecclesiastes 3:1

for every moment
we will spend dieting,
  may we offer twice as many
  to feeding the hungry;
for every mile
we put on the treadmill,
  may we walk more
  in the name of justice;
for every effort we expend
in improving ourselves,
  may we seek more opportunities
  to change the lives
  of those around us.

Presentation of the Lord – February 2

Therefore he had to become like his brothers and sisters in every respect, so that he might be a merciful and faithful high priest in the service of God, to make a sacrifice of atonement for the sins of the people. Hebrews 2:17

therefore,
    let us not hoard
the mercy poured
out on us, but anoint others;
    let us offer
the faith which
guides us, provide
    a path for
the lonely.

Annunciation of the Lord – March 25

Without any doubt, the mystery of our religion is great:
1 Timothy 3:16a

in the weakness
    that shatters our lust for power,
in the foolishness
    overturning everything we take for granted,
in the compassion
    which gathers the broken,
in the baby born into poverty
    who shares the riches of grace,
in the body broken
    which destroys death,
we are given the clues
    to solve that mystery
we call love.

Visitation of Mary to Elizabeth – May 31

The spirit of the LORD shall
    rest on him,
the spirit of wisdom and
    understanding,
the spirit of counsel and
    might,
the spirit of knowledge
    and the fear of the LORD. Isaiah 11:2

you carry
the Spirit which
  will teach us
  to transform hate into love
       and fear into hope;
the Spirit which
  will advise us how
  to become compassionate;
the Spirit which
  will open our eyes
  to the wonders of your
     grace, and
our souls will leap
with joy.

Birth of John the Baptist – June 24

See, I am sending my messenger to prepare the way before me, and the Lord whom you seek will suddenly come to his temple. The messenger of the covenant in who you delight – indeed he is coming, says the LORD of hosts. Malachi 3:1

when we record
  a book for someone with
  macular degeneration;
where we recycle hearing aids
  to folks we'll never
  meet;
whenever we spend our
  off days transporting
  rescued animals
  to their forever homes;
wherever we speak words
  of welcome and not
  turn our backs,

we prepare the way
to you for others.

Holy Cross – Sept. 14

Only in the LORD, it shall be
   said of me,
  are righteousness and
     strength; Isaiah 45:24a

while power is a commodity
easily brokered, strength
  is formed in your weakness;
while judgment is handed
down without regard, justice
  is in your hands;
while meanness is often
our way of being, grace
  is who you are.

All Saints' Day – Nov. 1

On that day this song will be sung in the land of Judah:
We have a strong city;
  he sets up victory
  like walls and bulwarks.
Open the gates,
  so that the righteous
    nation that keeps faith
  may enter in. Isaiah 26:1-2

as you open your heart,
  so all who have lost faith
  may find a home;

may we open
  our homes to the lonely,
  our workplaces to parolees,
  our churches to non-believers,
  our worries to your hope,

and we will sing with
all the saints who
did the same for us!

Thanksgiving Day

you shall take some of the first of all the fruit of the ground, which you harvest from the land that the LORD your God is giving you, and you shall put it in a basket and go to the place that the LORD your God will choose as a dwelling for his name. Deuteronomy 26:2

peace for nations
  and reconciliation for families;
hope for the despairing
  and healing for the sick;

wonder for the apathetic
  and joy for the sorrowing;
justice for the oppressed
  and new lives for the prisoners,

may these be
the first fruits we
offer in the farmers market
to the world.

ABOUT THE AUTHOR

Thom M. Shuman is a graduate of Eckerd College (St. Petersburg, FL) and Union Presbyterian Seminary (Richmond, VA). Currently active in transitional/interim ministry, his liturgies, poems, and prayers are used by congregations all over the world, and by individuals for personal devotions.

His Advent devotional books *The Jesse Tree* (2005) and *Gobsmacked* (2011) have been published by Wild Goose Publications/The Iona Community (www.ionabooks.com), as well as his wedding liturgy, *Now Come Two Hearts*. Wild Goose has recently published *The Soft Petals of Grace*. He is a regular and frequent contributor to the Iona Community's worship resources and prayer books.

He is the author of *Playing Hopscotch in Heaven, Lectionary Liturgies for RCL Year A,* as well as its companion book, *Piano Man, Poems and Prayers for Lectionary Year A; Where the Broken Gather* (liturgies) and *Dust Shaker* (poems and prayers) are based on the readings for RCL Year B. *Bearers of Grace and Justice* (liturgies) and *Pirate Jesus* (poems and prayers) are for RCL Year C. *Footsteps in the Dust* contains poems/prayers for Advent. All are available from Amazon.

Dusty the Church Dog and other sightings of the gospel is also available from Amazon.

He blogs at www.occasionalsightings.blogspot.com
www.prayersfortoday.blogspot.com
www.lectionaryliturgies.blogspot.com

Extracts from the New Revised Standard Version © Copyright © 1989, by the Division of Christian Education of the National Council of the Churches of Christ in the United States of America. Used by permission. All rights reserved.

Printed in Great Britain
by Amazon